GIANTS OF
BLACK MUSIC

GIANTS OF BLACK MUSIC

ORIGINALLY PUBLISHED AS
THE BLACK GIANTS

EDITED BY
PAULINE RIVELLI
AND
ROBERT LEVIN

NEW INTRODUCTION BY
NAT HENTOFF

A DA CAPO PAPERBACK

Library of Congress Caloging in Publication Data

Rivelli, Pauline, comp.
  Giants of Black music = originally published as The
Black giants.

  (A Da Capo paperback)
  Articles from Jazz & pop magazine.
  Reprint of the 1970 ed. published by World Pub. Co.,
New York.
  1. Afro-American musicians. 2. Jazz musicians.
I. Levin, Robert, 1939-   joint comp. II. Jazz &
pop. III. Title. IV. Title: Black giants.
[ML385.R59 1980]   785.42'092'2 [B]   79-27194
ISBN 0-306-80119-1

Published by Da Capo Press, Inc.
A Subsidiary of Plenum Publishing Corporation
227 West 17th Street, New York, N.Y. 10011

Manufactured in the United States of America

Foreword

Just as there is a natural adversary relationship betwen the press and government (any government), so there is between musicians and those who write about them. The musicians feel, most often all too accurately, that the critic or reviewer doesn't know the very grammar of music to begin with. Furthermore, these lay magistrates—who have much power over the economic future of the players—are often thrown off their soft centers by bold new sounds and designs for improvisation. In sum, the charge is that most writers on jazz listen backwards and sideways—but seldom forwards.

The only way, therefore, that musicians can set the record straight, for now and for generations ahead, is to speak for themselves. And jazz periodicals with the most abiding value are those that devote much space to interviews with the players: *Jazz Hot* in France, for instance; *Coda* in Canada; and, while it lasted, *Jazz & Pop* magazine in New York.

As you will note in this book's table of articles selected from *Jazz & Pop,* the majority are either direct interviews or pieces made up largely of extensive commentary by a player (most notably Robert Levin's "Sunny Murray: The Continuous Cracking of Glass.") And that is why this collection is going to be of lasting value. Just as I am convinced, for instance, that of the jazz books with which I've been involved, the one that is most sure to survive is *Hear Me Talkin' To Ya* (co-edited with Nat Shapiro), in which every single word is that of a musician.

Jazz & Pop, under the energetic Pauline Rivelli, ran other kinds of articles too, a few of which are here; but the core of its identity was its sense of itself as a place where musicians' voices had to be heard. Directly. This approach would not have been of any particular value, of course, if those in charge didn't know which musicians to talk to. But the presence of Robert Levin (*Jazz & Pop's* jazz editor) and of Rivelli (who had ears for a lot of then unmodish sounds) assured a perceptive series of choices.

During the 1960s, Robert Levin was a writer from whom I always learned something, and I still hope that he will return to commenting on and distilling the music. He not only had a strong background in the continuum of black music but his writing also had much of the passion of the music itself. And in a quick couple of lines, Levin could make sharply illuminating connections. As in the opening piece here: ". . . the New Jazz celebrates life, the new conviction of the black man. Depression being a symptom of internalized anger, try Muzak for a genuinely angry music." And he could hear beneath surfaces to tell you what was *not* going to happen: "A 'liberated' popular music, rock is, in many ways, a radical music, but it is decidedly more comfortable in the nature and proportions of its radicalism than is the jazz of the sixties." Because, of course, rock was and is white middle-class, and jazz is outside black.

Frank Kofsky, another *Jazz & Pop* regular, wrote of jazz in its societal context, recognizing that this music comes, after all, from insistently real lives that are shaped by economics, politics, and all the other intersecting dynamics of the world off the stand. But for all his immersion in the blueprints for a new society, Kofsky also responded very viscerally to the music itself and therefore could get to the actual people behind the horns. As in the interview here with John Coltrane.

Trane was usually most reluctant to talk about himself and about his music. He felt that if the music didn't speak for itself clearly, words wouldn't help. Accordingly, interviews with him are not exactly abundant. Kofsky's has a number of illuminating moments—as when Coltrane disdains the whole notion, cultivated by critics, that musicians can be neatly categorized into schools. "Myself," Coltrane says, "I recognize the artist. I recognize an individual when I see his contribution; and when I know a man's sound, well, to me that's him, that's this man. . . . Labels, I don't bother with."

Years ago, in much the same language, Duke Ellington told me the same thing.

There is much else of interest about the usually elusive Coltrane in the interview. His showing up at a Malcolm X talk; his incessant concern with mouthpieces and any other ways to further unlock those unheard marvels he was convinced were still hidden in his horns. And there is that poignant but enraging epiphany of failed communication when Coltrane, dismayed at the ignorance of *Down Beat's* attacks on his music, offered to meet with any of that magazine's critics and talk about it. There were no takers. It must have been an enormous effort of will for that shy, essentially non-combative man to have made the offer in the first place. And then the silence, the contemptuous silence.

What especially comes through in the Kofsky interview is Coltrane's extraordinary strength of spirit. Sure, he could get angry and discouraged, but his utter commitment to the music—to its infinite potential—gave him a rock-like center of gravity that kept him keeping on, one breakthrough after another.

The most recurrent theme in these interviews and essays is survival. What it takes—what it has taken for so long—for a black musician in this country to just function. To hope to be able to work at his music full-time. To have a reasonable anticipation of some kind of economic base. The most striking changes on these themes are in the piece on Sunny Murray, but there are overtones in the interview with John Carter and Bobby Bradford. And also in Pharoah Sanders's feeling-ful complaint that the way most jazz critics operate—not caring to find out why a musician plays his music—is "against the law of creation."

There is a particular genre of jazz profile that so reveals the whole gestalt of a jazz life that it affects the very way in which the reader listens to the music from then on. That is, he hears more deeply. A master of that kind of writing-feeling was A. B. Spellman *(Black Music: Four Lives)*. So was Ralph Ellison in his essays on Jimmy Rushing and Charlie Christian, among others, in *Shadow and Act*. Yet a third is Robert Levin in his exploration of Sunny Murray in this book. In fact, it is self-exploration, for Sunny speaks at length for himself with characteristic energy, vividness, and indeed, bravery. Although, to Sunny, the way he lives his life and convictions is not so much bravery as just his natural way of growing.

Even now, after so much of the history of black music has become known, most people—certainly those in positions to officially "define" culture—continue to speak of "serious music" by contrast with all the rest. "Serious" means, of course, white, European-rooted classic music. And all of the rest includes jazz. But Sunny Murray's recital of his uncompromising odyssey in black music—scuffling for bread in day jobs to keep existing so that he can keep creating—explodes the fatuous notion that this music is not "serious." It is, as is witnessed by so many musicians' histories, *As Serious As Your Life* (the title of Valerie Wilmer's book on black music).

But Sunny, like so many others, persists with everlasting resiliency. However, there is no choice but to continue, because this music *is* their lives. This 1969 article on Murray ends with what looked to be, finally, a clear shot at wider recognition. A date, under his own artistic conditions, for Columbia. But a footnote tells us that although the album was indeed recorded, it was never released. Yet, ten years later, Sunny is still hearing and sounding new possibilities, recording very seldom, greatly respected by a new generation of players, but almost entirely unknown to the nation's populace at large. An authentic creator of what Max Roach has called "America's true classical music," Sunny said back in 1969: "America won't be able to destroy us. We *will* be around—we're too strong."

In any other culture, has such vital and culturally rich music had to struggle for so long just to keep from being destroyed? That question is another obbligato to these essays and interviews. So is its answer embedded in racism.

One such battler, who did achieve some economic comfort until he literally worked himself to death, was Oliver Nelson. With his exceptionally penetrating intelligence, Nelson had no patience for euphemism. And that's why the 1969 interview with him about his African tour under the auspices of the State Department is so compelling. Whether he's talking about African music, tribal divisions, the extent to which American blacks can meaningfully speak of African roots, or how a government can control a country by radio, Nelson reveals the same piercing lucidity and silvery logic that characterized the best of his music.

Reading Nelson's report, which cuts a lot deeper than much professional journalism from Africa, I was reminded of something Duke Ellington said a long time ago and which I have often seen verified. It was Duke's view that since jazz players are very observant to begin with (the music coming out of perceptions as well as feelings) and because they are exposed to all levels of society, they turn out to be unusually astute travelers. Duke, for instance, claimed that as a result of his constant touring, he was pretty much able to predict political trends in this country long before the "experts" in the papers. So too Oliver Nelson in his trenchant account of his African travels.

The basic point—without romanticizing jazz players—is that they do tend to be more sensitized to all kinds of social interconnections than many of the rest of us. But this is a largely unknown dividend of the jazz experience unless the players are given a chance to talk about more than music. And that is what *Jazz & Pop* did make possible.

In another interview, with Bayard Lancaster in 1969, there is an interesting augury of what is now beginning to develop a decade later. Asked about women horn players, Lancaster says: "Oh, they could do anything they wanted to. In fact, it all goes back to the human mind not being developed . . . half as much as we can develop [it]. . . . You know, she just has to want to do it and not listen to what has been put down before." To which Marian McPartland has added that the problem in this instance has been the male conditioning of the female human mind as to who can or can't play jazz. Says McPartland: "If a woman has strong, innovative ideas, an original approach and a firm touch, people says she 'plays like a man.' Mary Lou Williams believes the reason for this is that years ago, women were not supposed to think. It was the man's prerogative to think for them and make the decisions; therefore, improvisation, which takes initiative, thought, originality and strength, was never believed possible for a woman to undertake."

In recent years, however, thanks to the annual Kansas City Women's Jazz Festival and similar developments around the country, women horn players, drummers, and bassists are becoming less and less a rarity in jazz; and I expect that if *Jazz & Pop* were still alive, there would be a good many interviews with these indomitable improvisers.

Some of the reporting in *Jazz & Pop* was also prescient. The 1970 article by Will Smith, "Chicago: Winds of Change," focused, before almost any other publications, on those improvisers involved with the Association for the Advancement of Creative Musicians. Players who are now leading the uncharted ways into the 1980s—Lester Bowie, Roscoe Mitchell, Muhal Richard Abrams, Joseph Jarman, et al.—are here illumined at a crucial point in their history.

As for my own contributions to this collection, I will underscore a statement by Archie Shepp in my piece on him because it serves both as an introduction and an open-ended epilogue to the book as a whole. I asked Shepp how he would define the base of the jazz tradition. Said Shepp: "Self-expression. And a certain quality of human dignity despite all obstacles, despite the enslavement of the black man and then his oppression. And each of the great players has had so distinctive, so individual a voice. There is only one Bird, one Ben Webster, one Cootie Williams. That's jazz—the uniqueness of the individual. If he believes in himself, every person is not only different but valuably different."

Coursing through these pages are players who, however uncertain their prospects, do indeed believe in themselves; and it is that thrust of self-assertion, whatever the hell anybody else thinks of you, that powers all jazz of value.

Shepp said something else that applies as fully to the present as it did to the time of the interview: "The underlying symbolism of jazz has always been black, and so have been the great innovators. But jazz is accessible to all people, if they're honest enough to receive it. Roswell Rudd in our band is an example of that. It's an honesty that's necessary not only in jazz, but with regard to the most crucial problem in America—the racial problem. Most whites have allowed the relationship between the races to deteriorate, but there are some who are honest about what has to be done and who do see the need for profound and meaningful changes in this country to end racism. But there's so much distance now between the white and black worlds, so much non-communication. And yet if that problem isn't solved, the future is, to say the least, very bleak."

The last part of Shepp's comment is, for that matter, even more applicable to the present that it was in 1968. The distance between white and black worlds has grown and deepened and, in a way, jazz— as used to be the case in the 1920s and 1930s—is once again one of the few terrains where some communication does take place. I have more than considerable doubts as to whether music can ever encourage basic social change, but John Coltrane may have been right when he told Frank Kofsky: "I think music is an instrument. It can create the initial thought patterns that can change the thinking of the people."

If any music can do that, it is jazz—because its own naked honesty requires equally open responses. Or, as Gato Barbieri once told me, "An artist can never be a revolutionary, except in his art. If an artist tries to be a political revolutionary, he will abuse his art. Can an artist at least *help* make a revolution? No, you can bring revolution into your art, but you can't make a revolution with art. The revolution has to come by political means. But perhaps the music can help people begin to change a little bit—begin to change in their consciousness so that they will be ready to move in other ways, political ways. Perhaps. That is all I can say."

And at least one can keep hearing that possibility—among so many others—in the music. Including the music of the improvisers in this book.

NAT HENTOFF
New York City
December, 1979

Introduction

THE NATURE OF THE MUSIC

One's first experience with the New Jazz (or New Thing or avant-garde or free jazz or abstract jazz or space music or new black music, as, with dismay, the phenomenon has variously and ambiguously been labeled) can indeed be disorienting.

Take, for example, the music of an early Ornette Coleman group which, in the fall of 1959 at the Five Spot Café on New York's Lower East Side, formally announced the most radical departure in the history of jazz.

For many uninitiated listeners on the memorable opening night, civilization had surely entered its terminal stage. To begin with (the impression was), four musicians—a saxophonist, trumpeter, bassist, and drummer—were playing, and with apoplectic intensity and near-intolerable volume, four simultaneous and very disparate solos which had no perceptible shared references or foundation. Moreover, even in and of themselves, these "solos" (to the extent that they could be isolated in the density of sound that was being produced) were without any melodic or rhythmic pattern, structure, or logic. Moved along by some invisible, capricious dynamism which was sending each man separate, and whimsical, instructions as to the tempo in which he should play, these anarchic eruptions consisted of ragged, disjointed fragments (or of long, directionless lines unmindful of bar divisions and chorus measures), and weird, aimless runs laced with strident, arbitrary honks, squeaks, bleats, and cries.

A number ended and another began—or was it the same one again? Impossible to determine.

But if, even after repeated hearings and critical explications urging the abandonment of outmoded, inapplicable criteria, a good many people continue to find the New Jazz imperious and opaque and hear only pandemonium, more and more people are coming to see that the New Jazz is as organic and inevitable a part of the jazz continuum as it is iconoclastic, and that it is among the most important and exciting expressions in the history of music.

Auguries of the New Thing existed here and there throughout the 1950s, but pianist Cecil Taylor's 1956 interpretation of the popular standard, "Sweet and Lovely" (for the long-since defunct but aptly named Transition label), was the pivotal record.

At the time Taylor was still largely obedient to the orthodoxies of bebop, the increasingly antiquated system which, in original and varied states, had dominated jazz since the early forties (inorganic tangents like "cool," "progressive," "third stream," etc., notwithstanding). But his "Sweet and Lovely" contained immediate indications of a transcendent music in which many long-prevailing, but eventually restrictive, systems, disciplines, characteristics, and standards of the jazz art would be drastically overhauled or jettisoned and the way reopened to the possibility of discovery and surprise which had been pretty well exhausted in the bebop context.* The recording served as the precipice from which Taylor, and others (in multiple ways), were imminently going to leap into another reality. Indeed, by the early sixties, with Taylor's Contemporary album, *Looking Ahead,* and Ornette Coleman's *Free Jazz* on Atlantic, the leap could for all practical purposes be said to have been accomplished.

Although the New Jazz is many different musics, all of its idioms have been ignited and nourished by the new black consciousness, a serious and profound spiritual awareness, and the necessity to have a music that could embody and reflect the dangers, tensions, revelations, and emancipated energies of the times. Its various expressions include among their properties and methods: an existential notion of order; a preoccupation with the origins, maintenance, and development of energy; the notion that no sound is "unmusical"; (self-consciously atavistic) voice like timbres and collective improvisations which discard the European-influenced separation of soloist and accompaniment; and the exploitation (insistently, crucially, on *black-American* terms) of increased black access to European, African, and Asian traditions.

The aesthetic (and its techniques) at which men like Taylor and Coleman—and Sun Ra, Sunny Murray, Archie Shepp, Albert Ayler, Don Cherry, Pharoah Sanders, Marion Brown, et al.—have arrived, and which is comprised of many primal, but long-dormant or submerged jazz elements and qualities, as well as newly acquired concepts, defines not just a new style but a new sensibility. And the depth and scope of the revolution which these men have engineered has immensely important extra-musical, as well as musical, significance.

THE SITUATION

With the blues, jazz has been, in every stage of its evolution, one of white popular music's major sources of inspiration, material, and renewal, and the New Jazz is beginning to have an impact equal to that of earlier forms, particularly on the hipper rock groups. On its own terms, however, the New Jazz has been persistently unnegotiable; even more isolated from the sources of money than were previous styles in their raw, unlegitimized (i.e., "unwhitened") states.

Not the least of the reasons for this circumstance is the direct relationship, aesthetic and attitudinal, of the New Jazz and black nationalism.

---

* The late John Coltrane, whom LeRoi Jones called "the new generation's hired assassin of bebop," was to find a few more places to get to within the chordal context. Coltrane rescued the bebop form from popular co-optation and the dreary predictability and staleness into which it had been led by the hard boppers and (driven by dynamisms which were basically the same as those of the New Thing players) took it to the absolute limits of its capacity. Taylor and Coleman, as Jones also points out, were proceeding as though Coltrane had already completed his work.

For one thing, fired by an unabashed "pride in black," the New Jazz is determinedly an Art Music. As Nat Hentoff has pointed out, the New Jazz is not a music for "boozing to or propositioning young ladies to, [not] entertainment in the show-business connotation of the term." Consequently it is too "heavy" to book into nightclubs and, in its effusive vitality, unsuitable for uptight concert halls.

(The extraordinarily emotive quality of the New Jazz, which, in comparison to the primarily cerebral work of "European" avant-gardists, gives transcendent dimension and vitality to its technical audacity— and which has an obvious connection with black liberation—frightens and antagonizes many listeners. Equating strong emotion with hostility— the area to which their own strong emotions are limited—they will say of the New Jazz that it is "angry." But the New Jazz celebrates life, the new conviction of the black man. Depression being a symptom of internalized anger, try Muzak for a genuinely angry music.)

Moreover, New Jazz musicians are not so controllable as previous generations of jazzmen have been and resultantly alienate the jazz-business structure on a social level. An anecdote from Martin Williams gives example:

"On stage, one of the big, great bands was performing. Backstage, one of the most successful producer-entrepreneurs approached an important young musician. 'You want to know why I don't use you avant-garde guys? I'll show you.' He turned toward the stage where the distinguished bandleader had just announced his next number, marched out, and whispered another title to him. The leader immediately announced the change of program to the audience. The producer walked off and said to the young musician, 'That's why I don't use you guys— because you won't do that for me.'"

Still another factor in the economic difficulties which beset the New Jazz is the rock phenomenon. As Nat Hentoff has observed, each new generation provided, in the past, a "nucleus of listeners" for whatever jazz was current. Rock usurped much of the New Jazz's potential audience. A "liberated" popular music, rock is, in many ways a radical music, but it is decidedly more comfortable in the nature and proportions of its radicalism than is the jazz of the sixties.

It should be noted here that those musicians whose styles, consciousness, and emotional references belong to the 1950s and earlier have not, by and large, had a significantly easier time of it. While many of Jazz's oldest and most fervent champions have found the New Jazz intolerable, they have also become dissatisfied with the older forms whose dynamisms are without contemporary relevance and they, too, have turned to rock. In many respects the going has consequently been even more difficult for the older musicians than it has been for the revolutionaries, for they cannot claim even the gratification of pursuing a mission. The musicians who play within pre-New Thing frameworks— who are neither intellectually nor emotionally inclined to follow the path of the Taylors and Colemans, have been, with a few notable exceptions, compelled to enter either the rock or soul (i.e., black popular music) markets, or blatantly to compromise themselves in hack studio work or shallow, jazz-oriented cocktail music. They have been left to compromise even the integrity of remaining where they are by playing less than they can play.

There appear to be no quick solutions to the hideous economic situation of the jazz musician. If many pundits would look to rock (which opened a vogue for authentic blues) as a possible place to locate an audience equal in size to the importance of the New Jazz, rock continues to function more as a wedge against, than a route to, the New Jazz. The only hope would seem to lie in the increasing awareness of jazz on the part of blacks and the new pride which blacks are coming to take in the music. All prevailing cultural realities considered, the New Jazz will very likely have to find its basic audience among blacks, and indications are that this is beginning to happen. Until it is a fully realized actuality, however, the New Jazz musicians (though they will surely endure the wait) will continue to suffer financial hardships which divert their energies and make it impossible for them to get it all said; and *everyone* will be short-changed.

Hopefully this book—consisting of interviews with, and essays about, some of the new music's prime movers—will assist the listener's access to an extraordinarily profound and beautiful musical expression.

ROBERT LEVIN
Jazz editor, *Jazz & Pop* Magazine

Did Someone Say Jazz is Dead?
by Frank Kofsky

Jazz, as is well known, is dead.

And how do we know that, you ask?

Why, how else but from those peerless prose stylists of the underground press, those luminous musical intellects who have contributed so immeasurably to our understanding of contemporary rock by discussing groups like the Doors as manifestations of "theatre of the absurd" and "music of total abandon," and telling us of Jimi Hendrix, "after he hurled his guitar at the screen in a cataclysmic-volcanic-orgasmic finale we fell back limp in our seats, stunned and numbed." If penetrating minds of this caliber assure us that jazz is dead, then there can certainly be no debate—jazz must be dead.

Which makes me a necrophiliac, I guess; because I happen still to derive no small amount of pleasure from jazz music. Or could it be that the announcement of jazz's imminent demise—an announcement that has been made repeatedly in the past, always to be proven false—is premature? No, that particular heresy would be too great for us to harbor, wouldn't it?

So necrophilia it is. For the benefit of those other confirmed necrophiliacs, I call attention to four interesting albums that have provided me with considerable enjoyment.

John Coltrane, *Om* (Impulse A-9140). To jazz fanciers who, like this writer, have been bitten by the Coltrane bug, a new album by that late and magnificent musician is an Event with a capital E. This one, recorded in 1965 when the personnel of Trane's group was still shifting, is no exception to the rule. In addition to the superlative work of the Master himself, the LP shows off to good advantage the playing of tenor saxophonist Pharaoh Sanders, who had joined the band only recently, and the incomparable pianist McCoy Tyner, who was soon to leave it. The passages which feature ensemble "free" playing by Trane, Pharaoh, and flutist (it used to be flautist) Joe Brazil are particularly impressive.

Besides these aspects of *Om*, followers of the rock scene should find this recording of special interest, regardless of whether they are familiar with much of Coltrane's previous work. As its title indicates, *Om* evidences that jazz musicians, as well as rock musicians, have an abiding interest in the religion and mysticism of the East. (In point of fact, jazz musicians were involved with Eastern music and philosophies long *before* rock players "discovered" the East. Saxophonist Yusef Lateef was performing compositions with Middle Eastern instruments over a decade ago; which was just about the time that trumpeter Dizzy Gillespie was photographed jamming with Ravi Shankar in India. So, if we are to have any historical perspective in the matter, it must be admitted that jazzmen were there even before George Harrison and Keith Richard.

For that reason, this would be an ideal album for the rock-oriented listener with a budding interest in jazz to add to his collection. It demonstrates something that I have long believed (and frequently written): that jazz and rock are evolving toward many common ends, though not always via identical roads.

Pharaoh Sanders, *Tauhid* (Impulse A-9138). Much of what was said of the previous album would apply as well to *Tauhid*, Pharaoh Sanders' debut album on Impulse, the first recording from this major innovator in several years and the only one on a major label. Like Coltrane, who was once his mentor and still, I'm sure, continues to be a major source of inspiration, Pharaoh is intensely concerned with the musics of the non-white world; there is even a track on this album entitled "Aum," which is merely an alternate spelling for *Om*. (Other selections include "Upper and Lower Egypt," "Japan," "Venus," "Capricorn Rising"— indicating that Pharaoh, like many rock performers, is into the astrological bag as well as the Oriental one.)

While the entire album is remarkable, the consensus among those I've talked to is that the most stunningly beautiful moments occur during the latter portions of "Upper and Lower Egypt," where the rhythm instruments set up a fantastically moving riff, Pharaoh enters with his tenor wailing, as usual, two octaves above the "normal" range of that horn, and then takes it out with a lovely chant in some foreign (African, one presumes) tongue, revealing in the process that he has a delightful voice for singing. (My feeling is that Impulse should have issued this portion of the track as a single; it's more melodic than a lot of stuff that makes it onto the top 40.)

Apart from its Eastern orientation (excuse the pun, please), the album should be of more than passing interest to rock guitarists for the playing of the Canadian, Sonny Sharrock, who demonstrates that it is eminently possible to play "free" on the guitar without resorting to fuzztone, wah-wah pedals, feedback, and grotesquely high volume levels. A major album.

McCoy Tyner, *The Real McCoy* (Blue Note 84264). As with Pharaoh Sanders' *Tauhid,* this album, the first by pianist McCoy Tyner on the Blue Note label, is an extension of the musical legacy left us by John Coltrane following his tragic and unexpected death in 1967. From 1961 to 1966, McCoy was an integral part of Coltrane's quartet. Later, when Trane decided to introduce Rashied Ali as a second drummer, McCoy and Elvin Jones, the original drummer with the band who has here been reunited with his former mate, chose to depart; the way in which Trane's music was evolving was apparently not much to their liking.

Despite that—or perhaps *because* of it—McCoy and Elvin play a very important role in keeping alive the Coltrane heritage as it existed in the mid-sixties, around the time of Trane's *A Love Supreme* album. On this recording they are joined by tenor saxophonist Joe Henderson, who has assimilated much of the Coltrane musical language of that period without sacrificing his own individuality, and Ron Carter, normally found holding down the bass chair with trumpeter Miles Davis. During his own lifetime, Coltrane lacked the opportunity to develop all of his own ideas to their fullest. Fortunately, his art gave rise to a number of associates and disciples who, now that he is, sadly, gone, can work and rework his innovations until all of their possibilities have been exhausted.

Revolution, Coltrane, and the Avant-garde
by Frank Kofsky

Thomas S. Kuhn's *The Structure of Scientific Revolutions* (paper-back edition; Chicago: University of Chicago Press, 1964) is a work that demands the attention of anyone interested in a *theoretical* approach to the problem of how successive develop-ments in jazz music are brought about. Kuhn, as is implied from the title of his work, is concerned primarily with the abrupt replacement of one scientific theory by another, an event he subsumes under the rubric of "scientific revolution"; but much of what he has to say possesses, within the appropriate limits, immediate applicability to the arts as well.

Kuhn's point of departure is the proposition that science does not—indeed, cannot—develop in a smooth, continuous fashion, science textbooks to the contrary notwithstanding. The day-to-day activity of most scientists, what Kuhn terms "normal science," is possible, he observes, only so long as they have at their fingertips a model ("paradigm") of their particular portion of the universe adequate to explain the phenomena considered of key importance (since no paradigm ever suffices to explain all the phenomena). Sooner or later, however, certain crucial data accumulate which disagree with the predictions of the paradigm. When enough of these significant anomalies have emerged, the authority of the old paradigm becomes undermined and the science enters a phase of crisis. (Though Kuhn does not attempt to deal with the question of what imparts decisive weight to a particular anomaly or set of anomalies, beyond remarking that not all discrepancies are perceived as crucial, it seems a straightforward conclusion that such deficiences of theory are likely to seem acute when they begin to act as the principal obstruction to a society's further economic-technological advance-ment. This would be why, for example, the 150-year revolution in astronomy, beginning with Copernicus and ending with Isaac Newton, occurred in the seventeenth century and not, say, in the tenth or the twentieth. For a more thorough discussion, see Herbert Butterfield, *The Origins of Modern Science* (paperback edition; New York: Collier Books, 1962).

The hallmark of a crisis period in science stems from the fact that the previously accepted paradigm can no longer be looked to for an account of critically important natural phenomena, while there is as yet no single new one which can serve as an adequate replacement. In this fluid situation, numerous theoretical innova-tions will be propounded, and their various adherents will be in competition with each other in proselytizing to secure the allegiance of the remainder of the scientific community. The crisis is ultimately resolved when one of the novel paradigms thus proposed wins the approval of the majority of practicing scientists and "normal science" once again becomes the order of the day. The rapid and discontinuous shift in paradigm that has eventuated is nothing more or less than a "scientific revolution."

Yet the matter does not end here, for the physical universe—that is, the universe as viewed by the scientist—is never the same after the revolution as before. One result of discarding the old paradigm for the new is that some problems that were held to be legitimate before the revolution are relegated to the status of pseudoproblems after it. (Astrology becomes scientifically disreputable after Newton, alchemy, following the chemical revolution which overthrew phlogiston theory in the eighteenth century.) But not every scientist is able to make the transition to the new paradigm with equal ease. Specifically, those older scientists who have done the greater part of their life's work under the old paradigm will generally have extremely strong emotional connections with it, which some of them may be unable to surrender. They may in consequence be ostracized by their former fellows and hounded out of the community of scientists. But in any event, the final outcome is to ensure the triumph of the revolution and the concepts associated with it. Subsequently, the revolutionary origins of these concepts will be quietly effaced by textbook writers in the interest of presenting a roseate picture of uninterrupted and unilinear scientific progress to students beginning their education; and all subsequent orthodox scientific activity will—until the inescapable next revolution—take place within the boundaries implicitly set by the newly ensconced paradigm. (In the wake of Newton's achievement of accounting for planetary motion by countervailing gravitational and centrifugal forces, attention waned from the question of what *caused* gravity—although this had occupied such of Newton's predecessors as William Gilbert and Johannes Kepler—and refocused on an examination of the *effects* of gravitational attraction. It was only in the twentieth century, when the paradigm formulated by Einstein and others overthrew that of Newton, that the former problem resumed its pre-Newtonian scientific primacy.)

Now, admittedly all of this may *seem* far removed from the world of jazz; but the distance, as I shall endeavor to demonstrate, is more apparent than real. As an illustration, take the concept of an aesthetic revolution as a shift in paradigm: surely there is no more succinct or precise way (once the terminology has been mastered) of describing the momentous changes wrought by Charlie Parker, Dizzy Gillespie, Thelonious Monk (and others) in the early forties in substituting a paradigm, bebop, based on harmonic improvisation with the metrical unit an eighth note, for one based on melodic improvisation with metrical unit a quarter note (swing). Kuhn's thesis similarly illuminates the events that transpired after the bebop paradigm became established. Younger musicians, who hadn't yet developed profound commitment to swing, were able to abandon it and immerse themselves in the new style with relative ease; but a sizable fraction of the previous artistic generation proved to be incapable of severing their attachment to the older music and remained with it; while the new canons of orthodoxy were then redrawn so as to exclude the veteran practitioners. That there was a subsequent reconciliation between revolutionaries and conservatives does not detract from the essential correctness of this (necessarily oversimplified) account, which draws on the model suggested by Kuhn, of the revolutionary and immediate postrevolutionary period in bebop's history.

There are, of course, rather patent boundaries beyond which the analogy between scientific and aesthetic revolutions, particularly as regards jazz, ought not to be pushed. For one thing, inasmuch as scientific hypotheses are evaluated on the basis of their success in describing objective physical reality (although Professor Kuhn would probably disagree with this statement), science possesses a fixed criterion for choosing between rival paradigms which jazz and every other art lacks. And while perhaps the majority of jazz critics continue to remain in blissful ignorance on this point, the truth of the matter is that there simply is no absolute frame of reference which permits one unequivocally to assert that this artistic idiom is "better" and that one "worse," any more than one can decide the ancient question of whether it is the landscape which is moving by the train or the train moving by the landscape (or both).

Another notable difference between the two kinds of revolution, especially in the short run, stems from the substantial amount of independence which scientists, in comparison to artists, have come to enjoy in determining the fate of a proposed paradigm, its acceptance or rejection. By virtue of a three-thousand-year history from which to learn, it is beginning to be appreciated that attempts to dictate the contents of scientific theories from without—whether as in the case of Platonic theological astronomy, American eugenics in the early twentieth century, or Lysenkoism in the Soviet Union more recently—have invariably been disastrous for further development. (The amount of scientific independence in any country, however, ought not be overestimated. Societies have found ways, usually indirect, of making certain that scientific research—as differentiated from scientific theory—be geared in directions acceptable to the politically dominant economic groups.) The jazz musician, on the other hand, enjoys no such privilege. This is especially true in the event of a revolution. Granted that such intellectual upheavals can be marked by acrimoniousness in the best of circumstances, the scientist is not additionally encumbered by having mutually hostile groups of critics, recording-company executives, promoters, nightclub owners, and the like enter the fray in order to defend their own particularistic economic interests. It is highly unlikely that these extraneous participants alter the outcome of a jazz revolution much one way or another over the long haul, since only acceptance by the community of musicians can assure the viability of a new paradigm; in this respect, the arts and the sciences are similar. Nonetheless, by the very fact that these groups are all, to one degree or another, parasites of the jazz musician's art, their eagerness to take sides in a revolutionary situation cannot help but obscure the genuine issues at stake, exacerbate antagonisms and, to that extent, obstruct the efforts of the musicians themselves to heal the breach. To see these processes in action, we need look no further than the avant-garde revolution in jazz which is under way as I write these words.

(It must also be understood that, in contrast to the conditions which prevail in the sciences, an older paradigm in the arts can be maintained by a dedicated lay public even after the attention of the most talented members of the artistic community has long since progressed beyond it; *vide* European painting and composed music as excellent instances in point. The net result is to render aesthetic revolutions more diffuse and less thoroughgoing than those that take place in science, and consequently more difficult to detect.)

It is this same avant-garde revolution which is my present subject and to which I wish to apply the concepts of Kuhn set forth previously. If it were the bebop paradigm, in all its variegated manifestations, which issued from the successful jazz revolution of the forties, it should by now have become abundantly clear that this paradigm has been seriously crippled—probably beyond recovery. Does this mean, then, that a successor paradigm has already emerged? While it is personally tempting to give a "yes" answer, on balance a more judicious response would almost have to be in the negative. The jazz avant-garde has firmed up its ranks and gained immeasurably in self-confidence, in my estimation, since last I had occasion to express myself publicly on the topic in 1962; still, one would be compelled to do more than a little violence in order to force its myriad and diverse styles to conform to a single pattern. What we have to deal with instead is the state of affairs which, were it to occur in one of the sciences, would fit nicely into Kuhn's model of the crisis situation: breakdown of the old paradigm, numerous new contenders in various states of perfection being offered to fill the vacuum, but as yet no single idiom dominant.

Supposing this diagnosis to be correct, it sheds some light on recent trends in jazz. Leonard Feather has correctly called attention (in his article in *Down Beat Music '65*) to the ambivalence of musicians and critics alike when faced with the necessity of pronouncing judgment on Ornette Coleman. But despite Feather's strictures, these responses to Coleman are not to be dismissed as mere "fence-sitting" (Feather's term), for they are entirely predictable reactions, *given the fact that the "normal" standards of evaluation have been largely destroyed without a substitute having been found.* Lacking any firm criteria for deciding one way or another, the majority of both musicians and critics, not surprisingly, equivocate, vacillate, and contradict themselves repeatedly. Far from demonstrating the superiority of musician-critics over their amateur brothers ("the musician," Feather informs us, "is less likely to be fooled into believing a bad performance is good"—which might be a valid assumption provided only that the musicians themselves could arrive at a working consensus as to what constituted "good" or "bad" in jazz), Feather's citations tend to indicate that the bulk of musicians and critics alike are wandering over uncharted terrain desperately in search of some fixed landmarks. But these landmarks will be discovered only when there emerges a new paradigm that obtains the approval of a significant portion of the community of musicians.

(Since Feather has, prior to very recently, been among the most vociferous of the critics opposed to the avant-garde—in 1962, for example, he condemned the avant-garde for playing "anti-jazz," alleged, wrongly, that the attitude of "most musicians" toward it was "generally negative," and concluded that "the last real jazz revolution" was "the arrival of bop"—a word more may be devoted to his latest writings. In openly admitting that "in the 1960s we have a curious [and why curious?—F. K.] parallel with the events of twenty years ago," he is on immeasurably firmer ground than in his anti-"anti-jazz" fulminations. But Feather has never accounted for his sudden conversion which, in light of the outspoken nature of his earlier polemics, remains unsatisfying for that reason. His readers have a right to know the motivation behind this radical change of mind; especially, one wonders if there is not at the root of the matter his frequent employment as a writer of album commentaries for Blue Note Records, a company that has been producing albums by the avant-garde at a prodigious rate during the past few months.)

Because it is characterized by no single dominant style, it does not at all follow that we can do nothing whatsoever about the avant-garde. For even if we cannot be exhaustive about what the avant-garde *is*, we need not be so hesitant in proclaiming what it is not. And one of the things which it very definitely is not is *atonal*. Quite often avant-garde improvisations are *nondiatonic*—i.e., depart from the fixed scales found on a tempered piano—but this is not to be confused with atonality, the absence of a tonal center (or centers). Incidentally, the writer most responsible for perpetrating confusion between the two, Martin Williams, appears finally to have been able to draw the distinction between atonality and nondiatonicity. Apropos of Ornette Coleman, whose playing Williams has been in the habit of describing as atonal, he remarks that: "Sometimes he isn't free enough, you know, because *he always plays modally*. People say he's too free—no he's not, *he's always right in that key*." (From a discussion of the jazz avant-garde in *Down Beat Music '65;* emphasis added.) We will return to Williams and some of his more idiosyncratic views.

As long as misconceptions are being dispelled, it might be worthwhile to make the further observation that, despite the sheer mass of verbiage devoted to him in the jazz press (and not only there), the single most influential figure on (and in) the avant-garde is not Coleman but— John Coltrane. Inasmuch as this notion may come as a revelation to some, the evidence for it—which is more than ample—merits examination in some detail. A negative confirmation, e.g., might be inferred from the fact that the initial diatribe against "anti-jazz" had Coltrane's group, which at the time included Eric Dolphy, rather than Coleman as its principal target. But before following out this theme, I want to focus on certain aspects of Coltrane's career previous to about 1961, a date that marks a rough watershed in his transformation into a member of the avant-garde.

One could hardly find a better example than the contrast between Coltrane's development before and after 1961 to buttress the thesis (inspired by Kuhn) that art *of necessity* proceeds by revolution. Although it has yet to be widely realized, what Coltrane was in actuality involved in up until that time was the attempt to carry jazz improvisation forward by a nonrevolutionary utilization of the basic bebop conventions. Consider: Coltrane's musical apprenticeship was served out under the bebop masters—Dizzy Gillespie, Thelonious Monk, Miles Davis. And if, as maintained by André Hodeir (in *Jazz: Its Evolution and Essence*), bebop may be schematically characterized as utilizing the eighth note in place of the quarter note of swing, harmonic rather than melodic improvisation, and more involved chordal progressions than was standard in the large swing bands, then the inescapable concomitant is that Coltrane was, as late as the end of the fifties, seeking to push the devices instituted by the bebop revolutionaries to their logical, evolutionary conclusion; he was not striving to subvert these devices— even though that was the ultimate outcome of his experimentation.

Thus the Coltrane "sheets of sound" technique, which seemed to puzzle so many critical auditors in the previous decade, must be viewed in perspective as the direct successor to the improvisations of Charlie Parker (possibly this is what one commentator intended when he called attention to the "general essences of Charlie Parker" in Coltrane's style). Where Parker had invoked the eighth note, Coltrane employed the sixteenth; and he similarly augmented the melodic complexity by invoking more elaborate chords and a greater quantity of them. Of this stage in his artistic maturation—the analysis of which by Zita Carno in *Jazz Review* still remains unsurpassed—Coltrane has been quoted by Ralph J. Gleason as recalling: "When I was with Miles [Davis], I didn't have anything to think about but myself, so I stayed at the piano and chords! chords! chords! chords! I ended up playing them on my horn!"

These two novel departures—the sixteenth notes and the heavier harmonic textures—quite naturally interacted to produce the sheets of sound as the only way of "covering" all of the chords in the allotted number of measures; they also led to an original kind of rhythmic attack and phraseology that was as intricately challenging as anything played by the first generation of bebop musicians. "I found," Coltrane told Don DeMicheal, "that there were a certain number of chord progressions to play in a given time, and sometimes what I played didn't work out in eighth notes, sixteenth notes, or triplets. I had to put the notes in uneven groups like fives and sevens in order to get them all in." A number of critics—most notably, I believe, LeRoi Jones—have recently begun to call attention to the fundamental role which changing conceptions of rhythm have played in the evolution of jazz styles. If for no other reason than the immense advance in rhythmic sophistication which they heralded, Coltrane's sheets of sound belong in the front rank of contributions to the literature of jazz improvisation, notwithstanding their having gone largely unsung in critical annals.

Most jazz musicians—or most scientists—would be more than content to be able to lay claim to a single major innovation in their lifetime; Coltrane's name is rightly associated with several. Having brought the sheets of sound technique to perfection in the latter fifties, he was forced to let them drop very shortly thereafter. To believe that this decision was due merely to capriciousness would be to misunderstand it indeed. Thus far I have avoided mention of what is surely one of the most controversial topics in jazz criticism: the ultimate causal agents which provide the driving force for aesthetic change. Comprehension of the in-progress jazz revolution and Coltrane's position within it requires that a few words be now directed to that unwieldy subject.

Viewed from one aspect, the history of jazz may be treated as the continuous (which is not to say uniform) emancipation of the soloist from the accompanying rhythmic-harmonic framework. Bebop, in this approach, would then be perceived as a set of inventions whose net result was to make the rhythmic pulse more subtle (by removing the steady beat of the bass drum and the pianist's left hand) and to widen the harmonic horizons (through employment of the upper intervals of a chord), thereby giving the soloist additional freedom. Admittedly speculative, my hypothesis is that Coltrane's extension of accepted bebop practice, crystallized in the sheets of sound, had, paradoxically enough, just the opposite effect: the dense harmonic matrix and tremendously rapid speeds of execution necessary to refer to the numerous progressions threatened to smother the soloist beneath their combined weight. Only a supremely gifted creator—only a Coltrane, in short—could hope to negotiate this chordal straitjacket and still emerge with something of value; and in the end presumably even he found the game not worth the candle. Implicit in Coltrane's decision to abandon the sheets was the conclusion that the daring improvisational procedures introduced by the bebop revolutionaries of the preceding decade had, by the end of the fifties, congealed into an artistic *cul-de-sac*. In that respect, bebop was no different from its predecessors: beyond a certain point, continued aesthetic progress became possible solely through the wholesale demolition of the regnant paradigm—and not by successive evolutionary refinement of it. (The parallel with the bebop revolution is rendered more striking when one considers that Coltrane, like Parker and Gillespie before him, was thoroughly grounded in the music that he subsequently did so much to undermine.) Nothing offers us a more direct verification of the applicability of Thomas Kuhn's conceptions to aesthetic revolutions than the sudden and wholly unexpected mutations in Coltrane's style that arose after he reached what quite reasonably could have been held to comprise the pinnacle of his development.

(Of course I realize that the foregoing impressionistic sketch leaves unresolved the more precise problems of historical causation in aesthetic revolution. Even if bebop ultmately had to yield to newer forms offering greater freedom of expression to the soloist, that does not in itself clarify why the transition began to occur in the late 1950s instead of half a dozen years before or after. I am myself inclined to accord primacy to a massive constellation of socioeconomic forces impinging on the urban Negro ghettos during this period: the movement for African independence; increased technological unemployment of Negroes; the consolidation of Negro determination to remove, and white insistence on maintaining, the second-class citizenship pattern; and especially the crystallization of overt black-nationalist moods on a widespread basis, etc. To judge by the relevant articles in the jazz press (such of them as there are, at any rate), the majority of (white) writers would not agree; their objections strike me as singularly unconvincing. It is universally conceded now that long-term social processes affecting the ghetto—the Great Depression, the rise of industrial unionism, migration from the rural South to urban centers, and the integration of the Negro into the industrial economy during World War II are the ones most commonly mentioned in this connection—were reflected in the drastic changes in jazz and other Afro-American musics in the forties. Why should this principle be any more outlandish when applied to the present era? Surely the fact that any broad movement of greater than momentary significance is shaped and channeled by the larger social determinants cannot be said to detract from the importance assigned to that movement's leadership. To point to the objective historical trends that find a partial representation in the current avant-garde revolution, therefore, should in no way interfere with one's enjoyment of the music, or reduce it to a "purely sociological" phenomenon. On the other hand, there is every possibility that appreciation and comprehension of an art will be enhanced by some firm *scientific* knowledge of the historically concrete circumstances out of which it has sprung).

Returning to the question of Coltrane's influence on the avant-garde, the evidence with which we have to deal is of three types. Firstly, an enumeration of his recorded appearances with various (other) members of that movement: Coltrane has been employed on albums recorded under the leadership of George Russell *(New York, New York)* and pianist Cecil Taylor *(Hard-Driving Jazz);* and the latter was most explicit in telling a *Down Beat* interviewer: "See what happens when Coltrane and I play together? He and [Eric] Dolphy can hear me." The linking of Coltrane and Dolphy, moreover, was not fortuitous, for Coltrane had on several occasions incorporated the later multi-instrument virtuoso into his regular group. Coltrane's remarks to the annotator of *"Live" at the Village Vanguard,* the second of a pair of his albums on which Dolphy appeared (the first was *Olé,* which also featured avant-garde trumpeter, Freddie Hubbard), demonstrate that more than a chance collision between the two men was involved. "For a long time," Coltrane related, "Eric Dolphy and I had been talking about all kinds of possibilities with regard to improvising, scale work, and techniques. *Those discussions helped us both to keep probing,* and finally I decided that the band was here, . . . and it made sense for Eric to come on in and work. Having him here all the time is a constant stimulus to me" (emphasis added). Finally the notes to his most recent release, *A Love Supreme,* inform us that Coltrane has recorded some selections with fellow tenor-saxophonist Archie Shepp, one of the out-

15

standing avant-garde luminaries. In all, Coltrane's collaborations with the avant-garde make up an impressive list, taking on even greater significance when one recalls how infinitesimal is the number of major artists who have seen fit to associate their talents with that movement.

There are, however, even more basic, if less tangible, manifestations of Coltrane's influence on the jazz revolution. Naturally enough, this is most apparent in the case of saxophonists, although by no means confined to them. As long ago (as these things are measured in terms of jazz's evolution) as 1961 LeRoi Jones, among the most perspicacious of the non-Establishment critics, wrote that "most of the avant-garde reed men are beholden to John [Coltrane]"; the passing of time has done nothing to lessen the validity of Jones's dictum. Jimmy Woods, Paul Plummer, Charles Lloyd, Prince Lasha, Sonny Simmons, Ken McIntyre, Wayne Shorter, Sam Rivers—these are a few of the musicians who could be cited as paying open deference to Coltrane on their horns. Archie Shepp and Eric Dolphy, whose careers, as we have seen, Coltrane has assiduously promoted, are also indebted to him for certain elements of their respective styles, but in a fashion more subtle and diffuse than with the other men. The number of saxophonists under the sway of Ornette Coleman to a similar degree is, I would argue, considerably less.

Coltrane's effects on the avant-garde have been felt even beyond the saxophonists' ranks. In *Jazz: Its Evolution and Essence* André Hodeir astutely observed that Charlie Parker's genius was illustrated not only in playing but in his choice of accompanists who shared his revolutionary concepts for reinvigorating the rhythmic-harmonic foundation over which the soloist spins out his creation. The same is true, *pari passu,* of Coltrane. His inventions in rhythm—worked out, according to him, in conjunction with the entire group—have been particularly fertile; even where they have not been adopted whole they have been of overriding importance in accelerating the emancipation of bass and drums from the fetters of a strictly metronomic function. I am at a loss as to why the critics have so generally tended to neglect Coltrane's contributions, when it would seem unexceptionable that they have played a momentous role in this liberation process; nonetheless, I have still to read the analysis which gives proper weight to Coltrane's use of two basses, for example, as an initial step toward shattering the orthodox timekeeping approach that, until extremely recently, was exclusively dominant. It is impossible to digest the work of such drummers as J. C. Moses and Sunny Murray except as offshoots of Elvin Jones, or an exceptionally "free" bassist like the incessantly iconoclastic Richard Davis without the prior explorations of the Coltrane rhythm section. For that matter, isn't it significant that Elvin Jones himself turns up with increasing frequency on avant-garde recordings these days?

It should not be astonishing that Coltrane's radical revisions of the jazz rhythmic conventions began around the time of his initial forays with the soprano saxophone. Even if Coltrane had not himself provided us with hints to this effect, it would be plausible to assume that the novel difficulties involved in working out a style on an instrument so dissimilar to the tenor, and one for which there was no immediately relevant modern jazz tradition in the bargain, would perforce have impelled him to make substantial alterations in his playing. Fortunately, we have something superior to intuition to go by. Interviewed by Bill Coss for the album commentary to *My Favorite Things*—his recorded debut on soprano, incidentally—Coltrane remarked apropos that instrument: "It lets me take another look at improvisation. It's like having another hand." Very likely the confidence of his soprano experiments and the diminishing returns from the sheets of sound fixed Coltrane's determination to pursue hitherto untrodden paths. "I've got to keep experimenting," was the way he expressed it to Coss. "I have part of what I'm looking for in my grasp, but not all." Patently the existing wellsprings of inspiration had been sucked all but dry. The same note recurs in all of his conversations on this subject. "I don't know what I'm looking for," he has elsewhere been quoted. "Something that hasn't been played before. I don't know what it is. I know I'll have that feeling when I get it and [until then] I'll just keep on searching."

Those who have stood so ready to condemn Coltrane for his relentless probing of the music's nether reaches might do better to muse for a while on the alternatives. An artistic style that once was pulsating with vitality may come, through nothing more than its unconditional acceptance over an extended time span, to appear incipiently moribund to a later artistic generation. By the end of the last decade, when Coltrane and many others were embarking on a root-and-branch restructuring of the improvisatory tradition, such was the case in jazz. It would have been more convenient, perhaps, if there were a new paradigm to hand as soon as the old one showed itself to be obsolete—but life is seldom that beneficent. Hence the only meaningful options that presented themselves were those of a prolonged period of somewhat random experimentation—itself the certain indicator of breakdown and crisis—or aesthetic stagnation; the most creative musicians (including, to a degree, Miles Davis and Charles Mingus in addition to Coltrane), naturally, took the former. Rather than indulging in their endless acerbic complaints, the jazz public and critics ought more properly to be grateful that they have these invaluable progress reports preserved through recordings (which is more than we possess for the early days of bebop). But that, I imagine, presumes an amount of enlightenment hardly to be met with in the jazz milieu.

It goes practically without saying that not everyone would concur with this diagnosis. The preponderant element in the critical Establishment, for one, would have us believe that the enshrined canons which have served jazz for the past two decades will suffice equally well for the next two. Such a static outlook is unhistorical in the extreme. It is contradicted by the entire development of jazz up to the present (not to mention being wholly untenable as a philosophy of aesthetic history) and for that reason is really beneath refutation.

Another point of view, advanced primarily by Martin Williams, displays a more subtle form of distortion. It maintains the genuineness of the avant-garde—or, in Williams' terminology, the "new thing"—but insists that Coltrane possesses no rightful niche therein. As I have been at pains to demonstrate, Coltrane is organically connected to the avant-garde by numerous and diverse bonds. Williams' thesis, therefore, is in direct opposition to the existing factual evidence; it has, moreover, inextricably embroiled him in all manner of indefensible logical antinomies. Yet because he is a writer not without influence in certain circles, it may be of some value to provide an abbreviated examination of his treatment of Coltrane vis-à-vis the avant-garde.

Williams' general critical stance derives directly from the fact that he is striving to reconcile a long and singularly uninterrupted history of derogating Coltrane with his own position as an unofficial propagandist for the "new thing." Taking the points in reverse order, Williams was, if not actually the first, one of the first writers to proselytize extensively for Ornette Coleman, beginning around 1959 in the pages of *Jazz Review* (and elsewhere); his 1961 article in *Harper's* likewise represented an initial effort to publicize avant-garde music outside of the jazz world and within the larger "intellectual" community. At the same time, his avant-garde predilections implied no sympathy for Coltrane's increasingly unconventional explorations. In the identical article in which he first proclaimed the merits of Ornette Coleman, Williams dismissed Coltrane with an offhand slur to the effect that "Coltrane invites the melodic disorder of running up and down scales." Three years later, in a review of Coltrane's *Africa/Brass* album, the substance of Williams' lament has changed but not its pejorative tone: Coltrane, he alleged, "makes everything into a handful of chords." (In reality, of course, two of the three compositions discussed by Williams were based on *modes*—not chords.) Overall, his verdict on the recording was that "if one looks for melodic development or even for some sort of technical order or logic, he may find none here."

When the teapot-tempest over "anti-jazz" arose in the winter of 1961–1962, Williams, in replying to the "anti-jazz" polemicists, took the opportunity to attempt to establish a separation between Coltrane and the avant-garde in the public mind. Emphasizing that "my opinion of John Coltrane's current work in no way reflects my opinion of Ornette Coleman," Williams by this tactic aimed at having Coltrane excluded from the "legitimate" (as determined by him) avant-garde. This was not in the least a fortuitous line for Williams to espouse; it was, in fact, the *only* means by which he could save face as an "authority" on the avant-garde, given his continued record of hostility to Coltrane. But, inasmuch as it necessitated a rather blatant misrepresentation of the actual relationship of Coltrane to the avant-garde, it unfailingly involved Williams in some monstrous inconsistencies.

For example, when Eric Dolphy in 1962 became a quondam sideman with Coltrane's group, Williams' problem became that of how to praise Dolphy, as typifying the *crème* of the avant-garde, while still disassociating him from his employer and collaborator, Coltrane. (That Coltrane and Dolphy regarded their music, at least in part, as a joint product is attested to by the quotation, given earlier, in which Coltrane discussed his reasons for having Dolphy join him.) Williams "resolved" this dilemma in the following terms: "Coltrane plays improvisations based on chord changes [sic]. So does Eric Dolphy, although Dolphy's fleeting departures from harmonic-orientation [?] seems to come more often [?] than Coltrane's." Yet barely six months previous to this, in the *Harper's* article on "The 'New Thing' in Jazz," Williams had reported that Dolphy "has said that he thinks of everything he does as *tonal and harmonic* (emphasis added). This was the selfsame Dolphy who departed from "harmonic-orientation" with Coltrane—and "more often" than Coltrane at that!

If for nothing else, one would have to admire Williams for his heroic exertions to have Coltrane denied admission to the avant-garde. In the essay on Dolphy and Coltrane from which I have already excerpted some of his dicta, the writer went on in an attempt to give the definitive *coup de grâce* to the idea of Coltrane as an avant-gardist by asserting that, "Basically, Coltrane's playing is conventional and traditional in its point of departure." Presumably, then, being "basically conventional and traditional" is mutually exclusive with belonging to the avant-garde. But in a subsequent paragraph of the *identical article* from which this quotation is taken, Williams sprang to the defense of Ornette Coleman on the grounds that—of all things—"a legitimate part of the jazz tradition is involved." So beneath all of this bandying about of "tradition," it would appear that the operative principle is: whose ox is gored? To compound the confusion centering around Williams' invocation of the two-edged sword of "tradition," moreover, consider a few of his choices in the *Down Beat* International Jazz Critics' Poll for 1961, held less than a year before his Dolphy-Coltrane article appeared: trumpet: Louis Armstrong, Roy Eldridge; trombone: Jack Teagarden, Benny Morton; alto saxophone: Johnny Hodges, Benny Carter; tenor saxophone: Coleman Hawkins, Ben Webster; baritone saxophone: Harry Carney; clarinet: Pee Wee Russell, Edmond Hall. And this is the self-announced prophet of the "new thing" in jazz! Well might one wonder if it is not a somewhat elastic concept of "tradition" that can be stretched to damn Coltrane and apotheosize Ornette Coleman at one and the same blow. Or further, if it is not more than a little ironic—to refrain from employing a harsher term—that a man who is so ready to disparage Coltrane as "basically conventional and traditional" experiences no qualms in selecting Jack Teagarden or Edmond Hall for inclusion in the Critics' Poll in 1961. Such gross contradictions as occur ubiquitously in the work of Martin Williams can, in the long run, only serve to disqualify his ideas from any serious consideration.

By this point the reader hopefully has been convinced of Coltrane's central importance with respect to the avant-garde. (Martin Williams' writings illustrate the consequences of affirming the contrary.) Is it to be concluded from this that his style will set the model for the avant-garde revolution? Put another way, will we, after a few years have elapsed, be able to refer to the jazz revolution of the early sixties by his name in the same way that we call the seventeenth-century revolution in astronomy "Newtonian" and the twentieth-century one in physics "Einsteinian"? As I have already indicated, the situation is still too fluid, the trends too mixed and uncertain, to allow one to answer with finality. It may not, however, be totally amiss to inquire into the subject a little more deeply.

It is in no way inconsistent with the tremendously exhilarating and liberating effect that Coltrane has had on jazz to observe that the bulk of the young revolutionaries have diverged from his footsteps in a multitude of directions; nor is this to be taken as signifying that Coltrane is "basically conventional and traditional" in his aesthetic. On the contrary, what we must do here is strive to gain a modicum of insight into the psychology of artistic revolutions. The avant-garde revolution is at the moment still in its infancy; the old restraints are in the process of being summarily tossed off without any new conventions having been found to substitute. In this "glorious dawn" we can hardly be surprised that all manner of weird, and in some instances actually anarchic, notions are being brought forward in the name of art. Doubtless just this sort of thing has occurred in every artistic upheaval of the past—surely in every sociopolitical one. Revolutions, after all, are notorious for releasing immense amounts of previously untapped energies and aspirations. Having just smashed the "dead hand of tradition," the youthful radicals are intent on savoring their freedom to the fullest; and, indeed, who can blame them for that? Moreover, the fact that the aesthetic revolution coincides with and partially reflects an incipient *social* revolution lends heightened urgency to the creations of these jazz insurrectionaries. (Don Heckman, himself a participant in the avant-garde, has observed that "Some of today's players conceive of jazz as a symbol of social change—even social revolution.")

When such symptoms of a crisis par excellence obtain, it cannot seriously be anticipated that the aesthetic revolutionaries will settle at once into any single new style, no matter how shockingly different it may appear in contrast to its immediate predecessors. That the avant-gardists are appreciative of Coltrane's monumental achievement in overleaping the stultification that afflicted bebop and its derivatives in the latter fifties is scarcely to be disputed; but that they intend to confine themselves to the path he has hewed is, for the time being at any rate, not a necessary corollary. For my own part, I would continue to insist that a good portion of Coltrane's work—his *Chasin' the Trane,* for example—is as "advanced" and perhaps more directly meaningful than anything else which the avant-garde has produced. But I can also understand that some of the restraints which the artistically mature Coltrane has deliberately imposed on himself (the use of modes as a basis for improvisation, the retention of a piano in his quartet) may rankle the more determinedly rebellious among the avant-garde. By no means is it precluded that the jazz revolution will come to accept the bulk of Coltrane's innovations in the end; along this line, I suspect that many of the seemingly aimless solos of some avant-gardists would benefit immensely were they compelled to develop against the sort of skeletal framework which Coltrane typically employs. Be that as it may, for any individual, whether involved directly or, like the author, merely a spectator, to maintain that this or that is the single road down which the avant-garde revolution *must* proceed impresses me as being the height of both folly and presumption.

John Coltrane
Interview by Frank Kofsky

In a review of *John Coltrane Live at the Village Vanguard Again* (*Jazz*, May 1967) I quoted a brief passage from an interview I had conducted with Coltrane in mid-August of 1966. By one of those grim coincidences that history sometimes seems to delight in, the transcript of that interview had barely been readied when word come of his tragic and unexpected death, 17 July 1967. In point of fact, the introduction which was originally intended to accompany that interview in the September 1967 issue was completed only on the weekend preceding his death.

I go into these details only to demonstrate that plans to publish the interview with Coltrane were laid well before there was any notion that he was ailing, much less fatally ill. That this must now be insisted upon is a sad commentary on the role of art in a business society, for business sees in the death of a man like Coltrane nothing more than an opportunity to hustle up an unanticipated few dollars. Thus, I learned two days after his demise that a major record company, having coincidentally recorded one of its saxophonists doing a composition by Coltrane a few weeks previously, was now altering its production plans so as to bring out the album as "a dedication to the memory of John Coltrane." It was this sort of disgusting eagerness to capitalize on what must be the greatest setback imaginable to the musical arts of the twentieth century, further examples of which are certain to be forthcoming, that gave pause to editor Pauline Rivelli and myself. Should we delete the interview and save it for a later day in order to avoid the charge that we too were guilty of exploiting Coltrane's death? Ultimately, we decided that the interview should appear, as originally planned. Regardless of subsequent accusations, our hands were clean. That being the case, it seemed senseless to alter previously made plans simply to prevent baseless charges being leveled against us, especially when such a course would have meant withholding from the world for an indefinite period what may well be Coltrane's last major interview. So the decision to continue with publication was made. Aside from the inclusion of my comments here, no further changes were made.

John Coltrane, the man and his music, means too much to me to let this occasion go by without setting something down on paper about him. I hope that what I have to say will be enlightening for the reader; but in any event it will be therapeutic for me, which is my main reason now for writing.

I am not a religious person, but John Coltrane was the one man whom I worshiped as a saint or even a god. I could never have written that when he was alive—if nothing else, it would have been too embarrassing for him had he read it. But since he is gone, no cause remains for denying it; and I feel that that tribute is the smallest gesture I can make toward acknowledging how much beauty and happiness he has brought into my life.

My veneration of John began, I think, in the winter of 1958, when I first heard him on Miles Davis' *Round About Midnight* LP. I was immediately hypnotized and entranced by his sound. If familiarity is supposed to lead to contempt, the process worked just the opposite way in my love affair with Coltrane's music: the more I heard, the heavier was I hooked. Especially so with his later post-1961 periods. Indeed, there have been times recently when one of the few things I could consistently rely on to convince me that life was worth the effort was the indomitably affirmative spirit that could be heard in Coltrane's recordings. I'm sorry if that sentence reads like something by Nat Hentoff, but that is the way I felt, and Nat and everyone else will just have to bear with me for the resemblance.

Meeting John in the flesh not only did not tarnish his appeal for me, it enhanced it. I do not pretend I knew him well. I met him shortly after he formed his own quartet in 1961 to the best of my recollection, when he played his first West Coast engagement at San Francisco's Jazz Workshop. It had been arranged that he would do a benefit concert sponsored by the Students for Racial Equality at the University of California, the proceeds to go to the Student Nonviolent Coordinating Committee. The concert itself was never held—the then Chancellor Clark Kerr would not allow us to raise funds on campus for the use of organizations like SNCC, which meant that there was no point putting on the concert. (Later, the Free Speech Movement was able to mobilize the Berkeley campus around this issue; but in 1961 there was not that much concern.) Nonetheless, it had been a very real thrill for me (as liaison with Coltrane) to carry Angeles jazz audience—I made it a point to seek him out and exchange a the cubbyhole that passed for a dressing room in the Workshop.

I did my best to keep up the acquaintanceship in the years that followed. I moved to Los Angeles later in 1961, and whenever Coltrane played there—which wasn't often, due to the backwardness of the Los Angeles jazz audience—I made it a point to seek him out and exchange a few words with him. Poor man! How I now regret robbing him of those precious minutes that he liked to use for catnapping between sets. But then I thought only of how I could manage to bask for a few extra moments in the presence of the Great Man himself.

In the summer of 1966, I was able to arrange for a two-week stay in New York to interview the leading musicians of the Jazz Revolution for a book on that subject. The name that topped my list, of course, was that of John Coltrane. In spite of a crowded schedule, I was able to persuade John to allow me to question him, a triumph that left me glowing. The circumstances of that interview may help explain the affection I felt for John and why the closer one got to the man, the more one loved and respected him.

There was no earthly reason why he should have consented to be interviewed, especially since it involved a certain amount of inconvenience for him. First off, he had to drive thirty or forty minutes from his house to pick me up at the Deer Park station of the Long Island Railroad. Then, since there wasn't time for us to return to his home if I were to be on the afternoon train returning to New York, he sat with me in his station wagon for over an hour, sweltering in the August heat and humidity while we tape-recorded an interview in the parking lot of a local supermarket (part of our conversation is inaudible on the tape, owing to the rattling of the shopping carts). After the interview was over and John had returned me to the station, he insisted on waiting with me on the sunny platform until the next train back arrived. As we waited, he asked me about my political philosophy (we had talked during the interview about changing the world for the better). He was thoughtful and attentive, when I told him I was a socialist and tried as best I could, given my nervous state, to explain the reasons why. And then the train came.

That, however, was not the last of John's kindnesses to me. The next day, I received a telephone call from Pharaoh Sanders, saying that John had told him I was searching for him (as indeed I had been, fruitlessly, ever since my arrival in New York) to interview. And so an appointment with Pharaoh was thus set up through the agency of John Coltrane.

I have never understood to this day why John went so far out of his way to assist a complete nonentity like myself. I can only surmise that, however much he may have had reservations about or outright disagreements with some of my ideas, he was convinced of my sincerity in working for a radical improvement in the human condition; and for that reason, if I am not mistaken, he put himself at my disposal. To say that his actions touched me would be the greatest understatement imaginable. But by then, I appreciated that John Coltrane was unlike other men: his humility seemed to grow in proportion to his greatness, and I believe him the most *genuinely* modest man I have ever met. (Those younger followers who are so anxious to try and fill his shoes with their own considerably lesser talents would do well to emulate the master in this regard.) It was the combination of modesty and human warmth that overwhelmed me in talking to John, and lent another whole dimension to my understanding of what he was saying in his music.

In the 1964 election, I wrote in the names of Malcolm X and John Coltrane for President and Vice-President. I mention this now only because I have been musing about it frequently in the days since John's passing. Then, I made that choice because those were the two greatest Americans I could think of. But now, I've begun to wonder if there isn't some hidden but nonetheless real connection between them. I think that there is. Both men perceived the ultimate reality about this country— the reality that you could know only if you were black and you were exposed at close quarters to the jazz club-narcotics-alcohol-mobster-ghetto milieu. Both men escaped being trapped in that milieu; both sought to use the lessons they had learned from it to show us not just the necessity for creating a society without ghettos of any sort, but also how to go about it; both, that is, exhorted us to make maximum use of our *human* potentialities, our reason and emotions. Neither was ever content with a static description of reality. Instead, both continually brought their most treasured concepts, assumptions, and definitions under relentless scrutiny. When these proved inadequate or outmoded, so much the worse for them: once their shortcomings became apparent, they were discarded like yesterday's newspapers. Such was the compulsive honesty of these two giants, the total dedication to truth at any cost, that made Malcolm X and John Coltrane the charismatic figures they were and won for them their large following of young people, black and white alike. Though cut down in the prime of life with their work far from finished and their best years perhaps still in front of them, it is surely safe to say that their influence is just beginning to be felt.

I was not close enough to John Coltrane to expound on "What he would have liked us to do"; it would be a cheap trick unworthy of the reverence in which I hold him were I even to try. Possibly there are others who have this knowledge; I cannot say. What I can do is to tell you what he stands for in my mind and how I feel we can make use of his life to guide us, now that he is gone. More than anything else, I think of John as a man who could never sacrifice what he perceived as truth for mere expediency, no matter how advantageous this might have proved. He refused to accept any single set of ideas as final for all time; for him there was no orthodoxy or dogma that could not be challenged. He was ever trying to probe deeper inside himself, convinced that if he could reveal the essence of himself to his listeners, they would be moved to do the same, thus developing their creative faculties to the maximum. He therefore required absolute and total honesty of himself at all times; and though he sometimes worried about the unfavorable consequences that such a course would inevitably bring in its wake, the hesitations were momentary, the decision to push ahead unalterable. If we are to be worthy of the music that he has left us, I do not see how we can do less than try to be as skeptical of what we are indoctrinated with as Truth, and as demanding of ourselves as he was of himself while he lived.

KOFSKY: The first thing I want to ask you is about a story that somebody told me. The first night I came here, the people I was staying with have a friend—a young lady—and she was downtown at one of Malcolm X's speeches, and lo and behold, who should pop in on the seat next to her, but John Coltrane. [Laughter.] Right away, that whetted my curiosity, and I wanted to know how many times you have seen him, what you thought of him, and so forth.
COLTRANE: That was the only time.
KOFSKY: Were you impressed with him?
COLTRANE: Definitely. That was the only time. I thought I had to see the man, you know. I was living downtown, I was in the hotel, I saw the posters, and I realized that he was going to be over there so I said, well, I'm going over there and see this cat, because I had never seen him. I was quite impressed.
KOFSKY: That was one of his last speeches, wasn't it?

COLTRANE: Well, it was toward the end of his career.

KOFSKY: Some musicians have said that there's a relationship between some of Malcolm's ideas and the music, especially the new music. Do you think there's anything in that?

COLTRANE: Well, I think that music, being an expression of the human heart, or of the human being itself, does express just what *is* happening. I feel it expresses the whole thing—the whole of human experience at the particular time that it is being expressed.

KOFSKY: What do you think about the phrase, *the new black music,* as a description of some of the newer styles in jazz?

COLTRANE: Phrases, I don't know. They don't mean much to me, because usually I don't make the phrases, so I don't react too much. It makes no difference to me one way or the other what it's called.

KOFSKY: If you did make the phrases, could you think of one?

COLTRANE: I don't think there's a phrase for it, that I could make.

KOFSKY: The people who use *that* phrase argue that jazz is particularly closely related to the black community and it's an expression of what's happening there. That's why I asked you about your reaction to Malcolm X.

COLTRANE: Well, I think it's up to the individual musician, call it what you may, for any reason you may. Myself, I recognize the artist. I recognize an individual when I see his contribution; and when I know a man's sound, well, to me that's him, that's this man. That's the way I look at it. Labels, I don't bother with.

KOFSKY: But it does seem to be a fact that most of the *changes* in the music—the innovations—have come from black musicians.

COLTRANE: Yes, well this is how it is.

KOFSKY: Have you ever noticed—since you've played all over the United States and in all kinds of circumstances—have you ever noticed that the reaction of an audience varies or changes if it's a black audience or a white audience or a mixed audience? Have you ever noticed that the racial composition of the audience seems to determine how the people respond?

COLTRANE: Well, sometimes, yes, and sometimes, no.

KOFSKY: Any examples?

COLTRANE: Sometimes it might appear to be one; you might say . . . it's hard to say, man. Sometimes people like it or don't like it, no matter what color they are.

KOFSKY: You don't have any preferences yourself about what kind of an audience you play for?

COLTRANE: Well, to me, it doesn't matter. I only hope that whoever is out there listening, they enjoy it; and if they're not enjoying it, I'd rather not hear.

KOFSKY: If people do enjoy the music, how would you like them to demonstrate it? Do you like an audience that's perfectly still and unresponsive, or do you like an audience that reacts more visibly to the music?

COLTRANE: Well, I guess I like an audience that does show what they feel; to respond.

KOFSKY: I remember when you played at the Jazz Workshop in San

Francisco, you sometimes got that kind of an audience which you didn't get when you played at Shelly's Manne-hole in Los Angeles; and it seemed to me that that had some effect on the music.

COLTRANE: Yes, because it seems to me that the audience, in listening, is in an act of participation, you know. And when you know that somebody is maybe moved the same way you are, to such a degree or approaching the degree, it's just like having another member in the group.

KOFSKY: Is that what happened at the *Ascension* date? The people that were there—did they get that involved?

COLTRANE: I don't know. I was so doggone busy; I was worried to death. I couldn't really enjoy the date. If it hadn't been a date, then I would have really enjoyed it. You know, I was trying to get the time and everything, and I was busy. I hope they felt something. To hear the record, I enjoyed it; I enjoyed all of the individual contributions.

KOFSKY: It's a beautiful record. It's probably the one record that I've had to listen to the most number of times to understand.

COLTRANE: You know, we've got another tape out on it now.

KOFSKY: What do you think, then, about playing concerts? Does that seem to inhibit the interaction between yourself, your group, and the audience?

COLTRANE: Well, on concerts, the only thing that bugs me might be a hall with poor acoustics, where we can't quite get the unit sound. But as far as the audience goes, it's about the same.

KOFSKY: Another reason I asked you about Malcolm was because I've interviewed a number of musicians by this time, and the consensus seems to be that the younger musicians talk about the political issues and social issues that Malcolm talked about when they're with each other. And some of them say that they try to express this in the music. Do you find in your own groups or among musicians you're friendly with that these issues are important and that you do talk about them?

COLTRANE: Oh, they're definitely important; and as I said, the issues are part of what *is* at this time. So naturally, as musicians, we express whatever is.

KOFSKY: Do you make a *conscious* attempt to express these things?

COLTRANE: Well, I tell you for myself, I make a conscious attempt, I think I can truthfully say that in music I make or I have tried to make a conscious attempt to change what I've found in music. In other words, I've tried to say, "Well, *this,* I feel, could be better, in my opinion, so I will try to do this to make it better." This is what I feel that we feel in any situation that we find in our lives, when there's something we think could be better, we must make an effort to try and make it better. So it's the same socially, musically, politically, and in any department of our lives.

KOFSKY: Most of the musicians I have talked to are very concerned about changing society and they do see their music as an instrument by which society can be changed.

COLTRANE: Well, I think so. I think music is an instrument. It can create the initial thought patterns that can change the thinking of the people.

KOFSKY: In particular, some of the people have said that jazz is opposed to poverty, to suffering, and to oppression; and therefore, that jazz is opposed to what the United States is' doing in Vietnam. Do you have any comments on that subject?

COLTRANE: On the Vietnam situation?

KOFSKY: Well, you can divide it into two parts. The first part was whether you think jazz is opposed to poverty and suffering and oppression; and the second part is whether you think, if so, jazz is therefore opposed to the United States' involvement in Vietnam?

COLTRANE: In my opinion I would say yes, because jazz—if you want to call it that; we'll talk about that later—to me, it is an expression of music; and this music is an expression of higher ideals, to me. So therefore, brotherhood is there; and I believe with brotherhood, there would be no poverty. And also, with brotherhood, there would be no war.

KOFSKY: That also seems to be what most of the musicians feel. David Izenson, for example, said almost the same thing when I talked with him. He said, well, we're saying in our music we want a society without classes, without these frictions, without the wastes, and without the warfare.

Would you care to comment on working conditions for "jazz" musicians? Do you think that jazz artists are treated as they deserve to be treated; and if not, can you see any reason why they wouldn't be.

COLTRANE: I don't know. It's according to the individual. Well, you find many times that a man may feel that the situation is all right with him, where another man might say, "that situation is no good for you." So it's a matter of a man knowing himself, just what he wants, and that way, it's according to his value. If he doesn't mind a certain sort of treatment, I'm sure he can find it elsewhere. If he does mind it, then he doesn't have to put up with it. In my opinion, at this stage of the game, I don't care too much for playing clubs, particularly. Now there was a time when it felt all right to play clubs, because with my music, I felt I had to play a lot to work it out, you see. But now I don't think that that was absolutely where it was at; but I had to find it out myself. It is a matter of being able to be at home and be able to go into yourself. In other words, I don't feel the situation in clubs is ideal for me.

KOFSKY: What is it about clubs that you don't like?

COLTRANE: Well, actually, we don't play the set forty-minute kind of thing anymore, and it's difficult to always do this kind of thing now. The music, changing as it is, there are a lot of times when it doesn't make sense, man, to have somebody drop a glass, or somebody ask for some money right in the middle of Jimmy Garrison's solo. Do you know what I mean?

KOFSKY: I know *exactly*.

COLTRANE: And these kind of things are calling for some other kind of presentation.

KOFSKY: In other words, these really are artists who are playing, yet they're really not being treated as artists; they're like part of the cash register.

COLTRANE: Yes, I think the music is rising, in my estimation, it's rising into something else, and so we'll have to find this kind of place to be played in.

KOFSKY: Why do you think conditions have been so bad for producing art by the musicians? What do you think causes these poor conditions that you've spoken of?

COLTRANE: Well, I don't know; I don't really know how it came about. Because I do know there was one time when the musicians played more dances, and they used to play theatres and all; and this took away one element, you know, but still it was hard work. I remember some of those one-nighters, it was pretty difficult.

But it just seems that the music has been directed by businessmen, I would suppose, who know how to arrange the making of a dollar, and so forth. And maybe often the artist hasn't really taken the time himself to figure out just what he wants. Or if he does feel it should be in some other way. I think these are the things which are being thought about more now.

KOFSKY: That's what I find, too. Do you think the fact that almost all of the original jazz musicians were black men and have continued to be throughout the generations, do you think this has encouraged the businessmen to take advantage of them and to treat their art with this contempt—ringing up of the cash register in the middle of a bass solo?

COLTRANE: Well, I don't know.

KOFSKY: Most of the owners, I've noticed, are white.

COLTRANE: Well, it could be, Frank, it could be.

KOFSKY: How do you think conditions are going to be improved for the musicians?

COLTRANE: There has to be a lot of self-help, I believe. They have to work out their own problems in this area.

KOFSKY: You mean, for example, what the Jazz Composers Guild was trying to do?

COLTRANE: Yes, I *do* think that was a good idea, I really do; and I don't think it's dead. It was just something that couldn't be born at that time, but I still think it's a good idea.

KOFSKY: This is true in the history of all kinds of organizations in this country—they're not always successful the first time. But I think it's inevitable that musicians are going to try and organize to protect themselves.

COLTRANE: Yes.

KOFSKY: For example, I was at the Five Spot Monday night, and I figure that there are about a hundred tables in there: and with two people at a table, it comes to about $7.50 a set, at three drinks a set. That means the owner's making $750 say, a set and he has five sets. And I know the musicians for that night aren't getting anywhere *near* five times $750, or even two times $750. So actually it turns out that these businessmen are not only damaging the art, but they're even keeping people away.

COLTRANE: Yes, it's putting them up tight, lots of people, man. I feel so *bad* sometimes about people coming to the club and I can't play long enough for them, because, you know, they're hustling you. They come to hear you play and you get up, you have to play a little bit, then split. Something has to be done about it.

KOFSKY: Yes. If it hadn't been for Elvin [Jones] taking the bartender aside, I couldn't have stayed there, because I had no money after a set.

Do the musicians who play in these newer styles look to Africa and Asia for some of their musical inspiration?

COLTRANE: I think so; I think they look all over. And inside.

KOFSKY: Do they look some places more than others? I heard you, for example, talking about making a trip to Africa, to gather musical sources. Is that the idea?

COLTRANE: Well, I intend to make a trip to Africa to gather whatever I can find, particularly the musical sources.

KOFSKY: Do you think that the musicians are more interested in Africa and Asia than in Europe, as far as the music goes?

COLTRANE: Well, the musicians have been exposed to Europe, you see. So it's the other parts that they haven't been exposed to. Speaking for myself, at least, I'm trying to have a rounded education.

KOFSKY: Is that the significance of those rhythmic instruments that you've incorporated into your group—to give it a sort of Middle Eastern or African flavor?

COLTRANE: Maybe so, it's just something I feel.

KOFSKY: Why do you think that the interest in Africa and Asia is growing at this particular time?

COLTRANE: Well, it's just time for this to come about, that's all. It's a thing of the times.

KOFSKY: Bill Dixon suggested to me that it might have something to do with the fact that many African nations became independent in the 1950s and changed the way Negroes in this country looked at themselves; it made them more aware of the African heritage and made them more interested in going back and looking for it. Do you think there's anything to that line of thought?

COLTRANE: Yes, yes, that's part of it.

KOFSKY: Another question along the same lines is: it seems that group improvisation is growing in importance—for example, what you do with Pharoah [Sanders] when you're playing simultaneously. And also, of course, *Ascension*. Do you think that this is a new trend now, or not a new trend, but do you think this is growing in importance now?

COLTRANE: Well, maybe. It seems to be happening at this time; I don't know how long it's going to last.

KOFSKY: Why do you think that's taking place now?

COLTRANE: I don't know *why;* it just *is,* that's all.

KOFSKY: But it is there—I'm not making something up when I say that?

COLTRANE: No, no, I feel it, it's there, but I don't know why.

KOFSKY: And another question about the new music: I've noticed that a lot of the new groups are pianoless; or even in your case, where you have a piano, sometimes you'll have the piano lay out during a solo, or during parts of a solo. Why is this coming about at this particular time? Why the desire to de-emphasize the piano or to give it another kind of role in the group?

COLTRANE: I still use the piano, and I haven't reached the point where I feel I don't need it. I might, but . . . Maybe it's because . . .

well, when you're not playing on a given progression, you don't really need it to state these things. And it would get in your way to have somebody going in another direction and you trying to go in another, there it would be better for you not to have it.

KOFSKY: It seems that the direction the horns are going in, too, is to get away from the twelve-tone scale—to play notes that really aren't on the piano; the high-pitched notes, the shrieks and screams. I don't know what words you use to describe those sounds, but I think you know what I mean. Sounds that were considered "wrong"—well, still are considered wrong by some people.

Now, if you play those notes that really aren't on the piano, and you have the piano there stating notes, do you feel that this gives some kind of a clash that you'd rather avoid?

COLTRANE: I suppose that's the way some men feel about it. As I say, I still use the piano. I haven't reached the point yet where the piano is a drag to me. The only thing is, I don't, we don't *follow* what the piano does any more, because we all move in our own directions. I like it for a backdrop, you know, for its sound.

KOFSKY: You do have the piano, though, lay out for a fairly large part of the time.

COLTRANE: Well, I always instruct the piano players that whenever they wish they can just lay out and let it go on as it is. Because after a while, lots of times, the pianists, well, they get tired. If you can't think of anything else to play—stroll!

KOFSKY: When I talked to you a couple of years ago in Los Angeles and I asked you if you would ever consider adding another horn to the group, you said probably the thing you would do is, if you added anything, you would add drums. [Laughter.] Did you have in mind then these kind of things that . . . ?

COLTRANE: I don't even know, man, but I guess so. I still feel so strongly about drums, I really do. I feel very strongly about these drums. I experimented in it, but we didn't have too much success. I believe it would have worked, but Elvin and McCoy [unintelligible].

KOFSKY: It doesn't necessarily have to be two drums. It could be drums and another rhythm instrument. That's what I was really referring to.

COLTRANE: I think so, too. It could come in different forms, shapes; I just don't know how to do it, though.

KOFSKY: After all, the things that you're using in the group now—shakers, bells, maracas—are rhythm instruments too. Not all rhythm instruments are drums.

COLTRANE: Oh, that's true.

KOFSKY: That's what I meant, when I asked you if that's what you had in mind.

COLTRANE: Yes.

KOFSKY: Speaking of Elvin and McCoy reminds me of something Sun Ra said, and I'll repeat it. I'll make it clear that I don't put any faith in it, but since he said it, and he told me to tell you, I'll pass it along.

He says that you hired Rasheid Ali as a means of driving Elvin and McCoy out of the band, because you didn't want them in the band in the first place, and that was your way of doing it. Do you want to answer that?

COLTRANE: No, I don't. I was trying to do something . . . There was a thing I wanted to do in music, see, and I figured I could do *two* things: I could have a band that played like the way we used to play, and a band that was going in the direction that the one I have now is going in —I could combine these two, with these two concepts going. And it could have been done.

KOFSKY: Yes. Sun Ra is quite bitter, and claims that you've stolen all of your ideas from him, and in fact that everybody has stolen all of their ideas from him. [Laughter.]

COLTRANE: There may be something to that. I've heard him and I know that he's doing some of the things that I've wanted to do.

KOFSKY: How do you feel about having another horn in the group, another saxophone? Do you feel that it in any way competes with you or that it enhances what you're doing?

COLTRANE: Well, it helps me. It helps me stay alive sometimes, because physically, man, the pace I've been leading has been so hard, and I've gained so much weight, that sometimes it's been a little hard physically. I feel that I like to have somebody there in case I can't get that strength. I like to have that strength in that band, somewhere. And Pharoah is very strong in spirit and will, see, and these are the things that I like to have up there.

KOFSKY: Well, strength, that's the word for the band now, strength and energy.

COLTRANE: Energy, yes. I like to have this energy.

KOFSKY: Do you feel that spurs you on, the presence especially of a man as powerful as Pharoah?

COLTRANE: Yes, all the time, there's always got to be somebody with a lot of power. In the old band, Elvin had this power. I always have to have somebody there, with it, you know?

Rasheid has it, but it hasn't quite unfolded completely; all he needs to do is play.

KOFSKY: That was my impression, too, that he really was feeling his way ahead in the music and didn't have the confidence Elvin had. But then, of course, look how long Elvin was with you before—

COLTRANE: He was there, Elvin was there for a couple of years— although Elvin was ready from the first time I heard him, you know, I could hear the genius there—but he had to start playing steadily, steadily, every night. . . . With Miles [Davis] it took me around two and a half years, I think, before it started developing, taking the shape that it was going to take.

KOFSKY: That's what's so tragic about the situation of the younger musicians now: they don't have that opportunity to play together.

COLTRANE: Yes, it certainly needs to be done. It should be happening all the time and the men would develop sooner.

KOFSKY: Don Cherry has a new record out, *Complete Communion*.

I think it's a beautiful record, and one of the reasons I think it's so good is because here he has a group that's worked together for a few months.

COLTRANE: Yeah!

KOFSKY: And so he knows how to put something together for all the men—it isn't just a "date."

Have you listened to many of the other younger saxophonists besides Pharaoh?

COLTRANE: Yes, Albert Ayler first. I've listened very closely to him. He's something else.

KOFSKY: Could you see any relationship between what you were doing and what he was doing? In other words, do you think he has developed out of some of your ideas?

COLTRANE: Not necessarily; I think what he's doing, it seems to be moving music into even higher frequencies. Maybe where I left off, maybe where he started, or something.

KOFSKY: Well, in a sense, that's what I meant.

COLTRANE: Yes. Not to say that he would copy bits and that, but just that he filled an area that it seems I hadn't gotten to.

KOFSKY: It seems to me, that your solo on *Chasin' the Trane,* that Albert developed some of the ideas that you had put out there and he had expressed some of them in his own ways, and that this was one of the points from which he had begun. Had you ever thought of it in that light?

COLTRANE: No. I hadn't.

KOFSKY: Did you ever listen to that record much?

COLTRANE: Only at the time it came out, I used to listen to it and wonder what happened to me.

KOFSKY: What do you mean?

COLTRANE: Well, it's a sort of surprising thing to hear this back, because—I don't know, it came back another way.

It was a little longer than I thought it was and it had a fairly good amount of intensity in it, which I hadn't quite gotten into a recording before.

KOFSKY: You were pleased with it?

COLTRANE: To a degree, not that I could sit there with it and love it forever . . .

KOFSKY: Well, no, you'd never be pleased with anything that you did for longer than a week!

COLTRANE: I realized that I'd have to do that or better, you see, and then I . . .

KOFSKY: I think it's a remarkable record and I also think you ought to go back and listen to it.

COLTRANE: Maybe so.

KOFSKY: Because I don't see any saxophonist now who isn't playing something that you haven't at least sketched out before. But maybe you'd rather not think about that.

COLTRANE: No, because like it's a big reservoir, that we all dip out of. And a lot of times, you'll find that a lot of those things . . . I listened to John Gilmore kind of closely before I made *Chasin' the Trane,* too. So some of those things on there are really direct influences of listening to this cat, you see. But then I don't know who he'd been listening to, so . . .

KOFSKY: After *Chasin' the Trane* and then *Impressions* came out, you did a sort of change of pace. You remember: you did the album with Duke Ellington and *Ballads,* and the Johnny Hartman album. Whose idea were these albums? Were they yours, or Bob Thiele's?

COLTRANE: Well, I tell you, I had some trouble at that time. I did a foolish thing. I got dissatisfied with my mouthpiece and I had some work done on this thing, and instead of making it better, it ruined it. It really discouraged me a little bit, because there were certain aspects of playing—that certain fast thing that I was reaching for—that I couldn't get because I had damaged this thing, so I just had to curtail it. Actually, I never found another [mouthpiece], but after so much of this laying around and making these kind of things, I said, well what the hell, I might as well go ahead and do the best I can. But at that moment, it was so vivid in my mind—the difference in what I was getting on the horn—it was so vivid that I couldn't do it. Because as soon as I did, I'd hear it; and it just discouraged me. But after a year or so passed, well, I'd forgotten.

KOFSKY: That's funny, because I think I know your music as thoroughly as any nonmusician, yet that wouldn't have been apparent to me.

COLTRANE: That's a funny thing. That's one of the mysteries. And to me, as soon as I put that horn in my mouth, I could hear it. It feels, you know . . . I just stopped and went into other things.

KOFSKY: The reason I asked that was because I recall that was the time you had Eric [Dolphy] in and out of the band.

COLTRANE: Yes.

KOFSKY: And there was a whole wave of really hostile criticism.

COLTRANE: Yes, and all of this was at the same time, so you can see how it was. I needed all the strength I could have at that time; and maybe some of these things might have caused me to feel, "Well, man, I can't get what I want out of this mouthpiece, so I'll work on it."

KOFSKY: You think this might have undermined your self-confidence?

COLTRANE: It could have, it certainly could have.

KOFSKY: Why do you think there's been all this hostility to the new music, especially in your case?

COLTRANE: Oh, man, I never could figure it out! I couldn't even venture to answer it now. Because as I told them then, I just felt that they didn't understand.

KOFSKY: Do you think they were making as conscientious and thorough an attempt to understand as they could have?

COLTRANE: At the time I didn't feel they were, because I did offer them, in an article in *Down Beat,* that if any of you men were interested in trying to understand, let's get together and let's talk about it, you know? I thought if they were really genuinely interested or felt there was something here, that instead of just condemning what you don't know

33

about, if you want to discuss it, let's talk about it. But no one ever came forth, so I don't think they wanted to know what I had to say about it. [Laughter.]

KOFSKY: I think it frightened them. Bill Dixon and I talked about this at great length, and he said: "Well, these guys, it's taken them years to pick out 'I Got Rhythm' on the piano, and now the new music comes along and undermines their entire career, which is built around understanding things based on those patterns."

COLTRANE: Yes, I dug it like that too. I said, "Well, this could be a real drag to a cat if he figures this is something that he won't be able to cope with and he won't be able to write about." If he can't write about it, he can't make a living at this; and then I realized that, so I quieted down. I wouldn't allow myself to become too hostile in return. Although there was a time I kind of froze up on those people at *Down Beat*. I felt that there was something there that wasn't—I felt that they were letting their weakness direct their actions, which I didn't feel they should have.

KOFSKY: Of course, that makes me want to kill all those people—

COLTRANE: Oh, man, you know.

KOFSKY: —because I get so much pleasure out of your music.

COLTRANE: Well, the test was for me. They could do what they wanted to do. The thing was for me to remain firm in what I was doing. That was a funny period in my life, because I went through quite a few changes, you know, like home life—everything, man, I just went through so many . . . everything I was doing.

KOFSKY: The perfect wrong time to hit you!

COLTRANE: Everything I was doing was like that, it was a hell of a test for me, and it was coming out of it, it was just like I always said, man: when you go through these crises and you come out of them, you're definitely stronger, in a great sense.

KOFSKY: Did the reaction of Impulse to these adverse criticisms have anything to do with those records that we talked about?

COLTRANE: The ballads and that?

KOFSKY: Yes.

COLTRANE: Well, I don't know. I think Impulse was interested in having what they might call a balanced sort of thing, a diverse sort of catalogue, and I find nothing wrong with this myself. You see, I like—in fact most of the songs that I even write now, the ones that I even consider songs, are ballads. So there's something there, that I mean I really love these things.

And these ballads that came out were definitely ones which I felt at this time. I chose them; it seemed to be something that was laying around in my mind—from my youth, or somewhere—and I just had to do them. They came at this time, when the confidence in what I was doing on the horn had flagged, it seemed to be the time to clean that out. And Johnny Hartman—a man that I had stuck up in my mind somewhere—I just felt something about him, I don't know what it was. I liked his sound, I thought there was something there I had to hear, so I looked him up and did that album. Really, I don't regret doing those things at all.

KOFSKY: You shouldn't. Johnny Hartman, in my opinion, went with the quartet perfectly. For a long time, those were the only six songs I knew the words to!

COLTRANE: Yeah, the only thing I regret was not having kept that same attitude, which was: I'm going to do, no matter what. That was the attitude in the beginning, but as I say, there were a whole lot of reasons why these things happened.

KOFSKY: Do you think that learning how to play the soprano changed your style?

COLTRANE: Definitely, definitely. It certainly did.

KOFSKY: How so? Could you spell it out?

COLTRANE: Well, the soprano, by being this small instrument, I found that playing the lowest note on it was like playing one of the middle notes on the tenor—so therefore, after I got so that my embouchure would allow me to make the upper notes, I found that I would play *all over* this instrument. On tenor, I hadn't always played all over it, because I was playing certain ideas which just went in certain ranges, octaves. But by playing on the soprano and becoming accustomed to playing on soprano from that low B-flat on up, it soon got so that when I went to tenor, I found myself doing the same thing. It caused the change or the willingness to change and just try to play as much of the instrument as possible.

KOFSKY: Did it give you a new rhythmic conception too?

COLTRANE: I think so, I think so. A new shape came out of this thing and patterns—the way the patterns—would fall.

KOFSKY: It seemed to me that after you started playing soprano, and particularly after *My Favorite Things,* then you started feeling that same kind of a pulse on the tenor that hadn't been there in your work before.

COLTRANE: I think that's quite possible. In fact, the patterns started —the patterns were one of the things I started getting dissatisfied with on the tenor mouthpiece, because the sound of the soprano was actually so much closer to me in my ear. There's something about the presence of that sound, that to me—I didn't want to admit it—but to me it would seem like was better than the tenor—I liked it more. I didn't want to admit this damn thing, because I said the tenor's my horn, it is my favorite. But this soprano, maybe it's just the fact that it's a higher instrument, it started pulling my conception, it really was headed into this instrument.

KOFSKY: How do you feel about the two horns now?

COLTRANE: Well, the tenor is the power horn, definitely; but soprano, there's still something there in just the voice of it that's really beautiful, something that I really like.

KOFSKY: Do you regard the soprano as an extension of the tenor?

COLTRANE: Well, at first I did, but now, it's another voice, it's another sound.

KOFSKY: Did you ever use the two horns on the same piece, as you did on "Spiritual" [*Coltrane "Live" at the Village Vanguard*]?

COLTRANE: I think that's the only time I've done that. Sometimes in clubs, if I feel good, I might do something like this—start on one and end on another—but I think that's the only one on record.

KOFSKY: What prompted Pharaoh to take up the alto? Was that to get away from—two tenors?

COLTRANE: I don't know. This is something he wanted to do, and about the same time I decided I wanted to get one, so we both got one.

KOFSKY: I haven't heard you play the alto. Do you play it much?

COLTRANE: I played it in Japan. I played it in Frisco a little bit, but I've had a little trouble with the intonation of it. It's a Japanese make, it's a new thing they're trying out, so they gave us these horns to try, and mine has to be adjusted at certain points where it's not quite in tune, so I don't play it, but I like it.

KOFSKY: I saw a picture of you with a *flute*. Are you playing that too now?

COLTRANE: I'm learning.

KOFSKY: You're always learning, aren't you?

COLTRANE: I hope so. Always trying to learn.

KOFSKY: I looked at the *Down Beat* and *Jazz* Critics' Poll two years in a row, and both years, this and last year, I noticed that European critics are much more in favor of the new music than the Americans. Almost 50 percent or 60 percent of them would vote for new musicians, whereas, say, only about a quarter of the Americans. Is this what you found in Europe?—or, in general, have you found outside the United States that your music is more favorably received by the critics, the power structure, shall we say, than in the U.S.?

COLTRANE: I'd say in the new music—and when I say new music, I mean most of the younger musicians that are starting out—I know that they definitely have found a quicker acceptance in Europe than they have here. When I started, it was a little different, because I started through Miles Davis, who was an accepted musician, and they got used to me here in the States. Now when they first heard me with Miles here, they did not like it.

KOFSKY: I remember.

COLTRANE: So it's just one of those things: everything that they haven't heard yet and that's a little different, they are going to reject it at first. But the time will roll around, the time when they will like it. Now, by being here with Miles and running around the country with him, they heard more of me here and, consequently, they began to accept it before they did in Europe, because they hadn't heard me in Europe. When we went to Europe the first time, it was a shock to them there. They booed me and everything in Paris, because they just weren't with it. But now I find, the last time I was in Europe, it seems that the new music—they've really opened up. They can hear it there better than they do here.

KOFSKY: I think that part of this is because what's happening in the new music is analogous to what's happened in painting, say, and sculpture and literature; and the people who appreciate jazz in Europe are much more aware of this. What do you think of this?

COLTRANE: Well, I don't know.

KOFSKY: In Europe, jazz is regarded as a serious art, whereas here, it's regarded as, well . . .

COLTRANE: Whatever it is.

KOFSKY: As part of the nightclub business. Otherwise, you couldn't have a magazine like *Down Beat.*

I know Albert [Ayler] is going back to Europe, and I know that there are many of the younger musicians who want to get away from the States because they just don't feel there's any hope for them here.

Do you remember Third Stream Music, what was called Third Stream Music?

COLTRANE: Yes.

KOFSKY: Did you ever feel much of an inner urge to play that kind of music?

COLTRANE: No.

KOFSKY: Why do you think it didn't catch on with the musicians? Was there anything about it that suggests why it was never very popular with them?

COLTRANE: I think it was an attempt to create something. I think, more with labels, you see, than true evolution.

KOFSKY: You mean, it didn't evolve naturally out of the desires of the musicians?

COLTRANE: Maybe it did; I can't say that. It was an attempt to do something, and evolution is about trying, too. But there's something in evolution—it just happens when it's ready, but this thing wasn't really where it was coming from. What was it—an attempt to blend, to wed two musics? That's what it really was.

KOFSKY: You said, talking about saxophone players, that there was a common pool that everybody dipped into. Maybe here, there wasn't enough of the pool for the musicians to dip into.

COLTRANE: Well, I just think it wasn't time. It was an attempt to do something at a time when it wasn't time for this to happen, and therefore it wasn't lasting. But there may have been some things that came out of this that have been beneficial in promoting the final change, which is coming. So nothing is really wasted, although it might appear to fail or not succeed the way that men would have desired it to.

KOFSKY: Even the mistakes can be instructive if you try to use them. Do you make any attempt, or do you feel that you should make any attempt, to educate your audience in ways that aren't strictly musical, that is, it's obvious that you want your audience to understand what you're doing musically. But do you feel that you want them to understand other things, too, and that you have some kind of responsibility for it?

COLTRANE: Sure, I feel this, and this is one of the things I am concerned about now. I just don't know how to go about this. I want to find out just how I should do it. I think it's going to have to be very subtle; you can't ram philosophies down anybody's throat, and the music is enough! That's philosophy. I think the best thing I can do at this time is to try to get myself in shape and know myself. If I can do that, then I'll just play, you see, and leave it at that. I believe that will do it, if I really can get to myself and be just as I feel I should be and play it. And I think they'll get it, because music goes a long way—it can influence.

KOFSKY: That's how I got interested in those things I was talking about earlier, like Malcolm X. I might not have come to it, or come to it as fast, if it hadn't been for the music. That was my first introduction to something beyond my own horizons, that would make me think about the world I was living in.

COLTRANE: Yes. That's what I'm sure of, man, I'm really sure of this thing. As I say, there are things which as far as spirituality is concerned, which is very important to me at this time, I've got to grow through certain phases of this to other understanding and more consciousness and awareness of just what it is that I'm supposed to understand about it; and I'm sure others will be part of the music. To me, you know, I feel I want to be a force for good.

KOFSKY: And the music too?

COLTRANE: Everywhere. You know, I want to be a force for real good. In other words, I know that there are bad forces, forces put here that bring suffering to others and misery to the world, but I want to be the force which is truly for good.

KOFSKY: I don't have any more of my prepared questions to ask you —or my improvised questions to ask you. [Laughter.] I had a lot of questions here that were related just to you. Many of those questions about music I don't ask of the other musicians; but I've always had a very special interest in your work, so I took this opportunity, since I don't know when I'll ever get the chance to get you down on tape again. Do you have anything else that you'd like to get on here?

COLTRANE: I think we just about covered, I believe, just about covered it.

[As John drove me back to the station, the tape recorder was left on and we continued to talk. After some humorous exchanges, the conversation turned to the proper function of a jazz writer or critic.]

KOFSKY: If you can't play the music, and if you're going to write about it, you have, I think, an obligation to do it as conscientiously as possible.

COLTRANE: Yes, I believe it, man.

KOFSKY: And always when it's a question of your opinion versus the musician's opinion, to give the benefit of the doubt to the musician, because he knows the music far better than you'll ever know it. In other words, you have to be humble. A lot of writers aren't humble; they get arrogant because they think they have some kind of power.

COLTRANE: Well, that's one of the main causes of this arrogance— the idea of power. Then you lose your true power, which is to be part of all, and the only way you can be part of all is to understand it. And when there's something you don't understand, you have to go humbly to it. You don't go to school and sit down and say, "I know what you're getting ready to teach me." You sit there and you learn. You open your mind. You absorb. But you have to be quiet, you have to be still to do all of this.

KOFSKY: That's what so annoyed me about all of that stuff they were saying about you in '61.

COLTRANE: Oh, that was terrible. I couldn't believe it, you know, it just seemed so preposterous. It was so ridiculous, man, that's what bugs me. It was absolutely ridiculous, because they made it appear that we didn't even know the first thing about music—the first thing. And there we were really trying to push things off.

KOFSKY: Because they never stand still.

COLTRANE: Eric [Dolphy], man, as sweet as this cat was and the musician that he was—it hurt me to see him get hurt in this thing.

KOFSKY: Do you think that this possibly contributed to the fact that he died so young?

COLTRANE: I don't know, but Eric was a strong cat. Nobody knows what caused it. The way he passed, there was a mystery about it.

KOFSKY: I didn't mean that it was directly the cause, but—

COLTRANE: Indirectly?

KOFSKY: Yes.

COLTRANE: Yes. The whole scene, man. He couldn't work . . .

KOFSKY: That's what I meant, really.

COLTRANE: He always seemed to be a very cheerful young man, so I don't *think* that would put him . . . I don't think so, because he had an outlook on life which was very, very good—optimistic, and he had this sort of thing, friendliness, you know, a real friend to everyone. He was the type of man who could be as much a friend to a guy he'd just met today as he was to one he'd known for ten years. This kind of person, I don't think it would really hurt him to the point where he would do something to hurt himself consciously or unconsciously.

KOFSKY: Yes. That friendliness was one of the things that has impressed me about the musicians here. I really didn't expect to be greeted with open arms, because I am an outsider, after all. And yet I have been amazed constantly at how eager the musicians were to cooperate when they decided that I was sincere and that this wasn't a joke or a con or something of that nature.

COLTRANE: I think all we need is sincerity, empathy. [After another digression.]

COLTRANE: I think I want to get closer to town. Maybe there's something I can do in music. Get a place, a little room to play in. I don't want a loft, but maybe there's something I can get to play in, just some place to be able to work in.

KOFSKY: Where do you play at home?

COLTRANE: Anywhere. There's a room over the garage that I'm getting fixed now and I think it's going to be my practice room. You never know. Sometimes you build a little room and it ends up you're still going in the toilet. I hope I like it, but . . . I keep a horn in my bedroom—a flute usually back there, because when I go there I'm tired and I lay down and practice. [!]

KOFSKY: About how many hours a day do you play?

COLTRANE: Not too much at this time. I find that it's only when something is trying to come through that I really practice. And then I don't even know how many hours—it's all day, on and off. But at this time there's nothing coming out now.

KOFSKY: I was very surprised to hear you practicing at all, because I just couldn't conceive of what you could find to practice! But I know it isn't like that.

COLTRANE: I *need* to practice. It's just that I want something to practice, and I'm trying to find out what it is that I want, an area that I want to get into.

John Carter and Bobby Bradford Interview by Frank Kofsky

KOFSKY: Where do you know John from?

BRADFORD: John and I knew *of* each other in Texas. Even though Fort Worth and Dallas, where we lived, are only eighteen or twenty miles apart, we never crossed trails until we were in California. I knew of him through mutual friends.

CARTER: I was interested in getting a thing going, and Ornette said, well, you and Bobby Bradford ought to get together because Bobby Bradford is here in California somewhere. But he didn't know where Bob was at that time, so he called to Texas, to a mutual friend of ours, and he had Bob's brother's address, phone number, so I called him. Bob and I finally got together like that, and were already working by the time of the big-band thing at UCLA, in 1966.

KOFSKY: This is just in passing, but it's of interest to me. Have either of you tried to work at all as studio musicians? Have you had any experience along that line; and if so, what sort of experience has it been? What have you found?

BRADFORD: I haven't even looked for any studio work.

KOFSKY: That hasn't interested you?

BRADFORD: It would have interested me from the part of making some dough, but I knew what it would involve. It would mean my devoting full time to the horn, you see, which would have meant like starting off from scratch with a family and trying to get into the studio bag, that's what it meant to me, conditioning myself to the gymnastics of the thing, studio trumpet.

KOFSKY: Which is different than playing what you play now?

BRADFORD: Oh yeah, it demands, you know, conditioning, physical conditioning . . .

CARTER: Not only that, but I had big aspirations for being a studio musician at one time, and there is a difference . . . You know, everything in the studio has to be very "legitimate," because you're called on to play all kinds of music and it's all got to be played quite legitimately.

BRADFORD: The way *they* want it.

CARTER: The way *they* want it. And it isn't in keeping at all with what we consider free things. My aspirations were stemmed because of the hassle of trying to do it, much as Bob says. It's a full-time thing, it's a closed circle that you cannot get into unless somebody really knows you and takes you in by the hand. Other than that, I don't know how you get into doing studio work; and

I soon became very discouraged with trying. I stopped, and I'm not sure I would have been happy doing it. I'm much happier doing what I'm doing.

KOFSKY: It has often been charged—and I wanted to check up by using your own experience, if I can pursue the point just for a second further—that it's more difficult for a black man to crack into the studio circuit.

BRADFORD: Oh, by all means!

CARTER: You can look at the number of musicians here in Los Angeles. There *are* good black musicians here who can play and go and sit down and read the music. Bob and I can go and sit down and read the music. But there are a handful of black musicians in Hollywood who are making a good living out of free-lance recordings, just a handful—and there are many guys who could do it. At the same time, there are many white musicians who are also excluded.

CARTER: So it isn't the fact that you don't get in . . .

KOFSKY: Exclusively because you're black; but it certainly is an additional handicap if that's your aspiration.

CARTER & BRADFORD: *Yeah!*

KOFSKY: Now that Black Studies seem to be legitimate, have either of you thought about or been approached to teach courses in this area by any of the colleges or high schools in southern California?

BRADFORD: I've been approached and I'm already teaching.

KOFSKY: Good! Where?

BRADFORD: Cal State at Dominguez Hills. [A black and brown area south of the central city—F. K.]

KOFSKY: I'm delighted; how do you feel about it?

BRADFORD: I am, too; I am, too—but it's a hassle, man. What I see, if the Black Studies thing is going to be legitimate, like you say, then it's going to be done like it is. The cats who are going to teach it are going to be, you know, people like myself, or like John. The material that I can get out of books to make available to people is available to anybody. I don't think the course is enhanced because I happen to have a black face. It's because I happen to have a little bit more of an inside view on what's happening, you know. In fact, very often I find I have to translate the records—"What are they saying?" It comes to that. Like, "What did he say?" Do you know what I mean? Some blues singer is singing and nobody understands what he's singing. It comes to that. Of course, that's not a big thing, but . . .

KOFSKY: But it's an indication.

BRADFORD: It's an indication of how far away the cat is from what's really happening.

CARTER: And this helps to give a person who is in that position a big insight into what's going on.

KOFSKY: What also interests me, especially after hearing the playback of the tapes you've just made, is how a group of this caliber could be neglected for so long in Los Angeles.

BRADFORD: We're not the only group.

KOFSKY: No, I know you're not. That's the thing I want to bring out. Your band is indicative of some kind of black musical renaissance in Los Angeles that simply hasn't been noticed, hasn't had any attention paid to it.

CARTER: First of all, there's no place for exposure. We've been playing where we're playing—in the ghetto—for a long time. There are only three jazz clubs in the town.

KOFSKY: Why do you suppose you can't get booked into clubs?

BRADFORD: First of all, if we were playing straight-up-and-down kind of jazz, it would help. But playing what we're playing, and not being the kind of music that the mass of people are going to rush into the club to hear, the club owner—being concerned with having a group there that a crowd of people are going to come to hear—is not prepared to take any kind of chance on a group like ours, where, if an owner is going to take a chance, they'd rather take it on a group that at least they are *personally* happy with. Do you know what I mean? Like there'd be no skin off a club owner's . . . I don't know what their books say, but I can look around and count the number of seats in a club and sit there for a night and figure out what kind of dough is there—it doesn't take any brains for that. So it wouldn't be a risk for the cat to use a group like ours on Sunday afternoon. The people will come out just to see people up on a stand with shiny instruments—they're going to come.

CARTER: The owners are not interested in promoting a new thing, new music and new groups and stuff. It's back to what Bob said.

BRADFORD: There aren't a lot of places in the black community where we could go and play—you can forget about black clubs. And the black clubs that *are* there: a lot of people may have the opinion that, well, surely, you could take your bands into the black clubs. But the black clubs operate on a *club* basis—just like the whites. The black clubs that are open are interested in selling the drinks and getting the cover. Now if we drew a lot of people, they wouldn't care what we were playing. What happens in a club in the black community, I think, like if we played there once for the management, the thing is, on the basis of what we were playing, he'd never test to find out if we *would* draw. What's on the jukebox and what's on the radio and what black people listen to on the stations that are black stations—

KOFSKY: So called.

BRADFORD: Yes—are things that everybody knows are in a certain bag. So if the difference, probably, between a black and white club—the political thing would never come into it. If we auditioned for a club, a black club, and if we played there one night and the house was packed —then we'd continue to play there. You see? I can't swear that that would be true in another club.

KOFSKY: It does show that the so-called black bourgeoisie doesn't have any more interest in developing the music than the white bourgeoisie.

BRADFORD: Yeah, how about that? What do you think of that, John?

CARTER: What did you say?

KOFSKY: I said the black bourgeoisie, as represented by the club owners, doesn't seem to have any more interest in developing this music than the white bourgeoisie.

CARTER: No. That would be a true statement.

KOFSKY: It also seems to me that there's a contradiction here and that the media of Los Angeles are culpable, in that they've gone to great lengths to publicize things like the Watts Writers' Workshop, in a vein of liberal paternalism, but they haven't made any attempt to publicize the indigenous music. So that while the white community at, more or less, large is aware that there's literary talent in Watts, there's no awareness that there exists comparable musical talent.

CARTER: I don't know why that is. But still, here again, you have to think of the matter of the art for art's sake thing and the matter of making money.

KOFSKY: The Writers' Workshop hasn't been a tremendously successful enterprise from the commercial point of view. It's basically a kind of white *noblesse oblige:* "Well, we're going to go into Watts and show that the situation is not completely hopeless, blah, blah, blah." Which may or may not be a valid premise, but the point is that they did that for writers —why didn't they do it for musicians as well?

CARTER: I don't know.

KOFSKY: It's kind of curious.

CARTER: I don't know how many people are able to listen to jazz. Music like we play—different people have many different things they think about what jazz is. I don't know how many people are able to listen to the kind of thing we are doing, and then decide whether this is good or this is not, or if it's artful or if it isn't.

KOFSKY: That's right. Any idiot can sit down and read a printed page and think that he understands what's happening. But with music, people seem to have a different frame of reference. If at the first hearing they don't hear something that they recognize or like, it never seems to get beyond that first hearing.

CARTER: Right, and, you see, the thing we do is the kind of thing that pretty quickly throws that person off. He doesn't hear the regular thing he can pat his foot to and shake his head. We're in and out of different things and so it's likely that a person who would hear us might not have a good understanding. He'd have to be really involved . . .

BRADFORD: I'm amazed now at blacks *and* whites who do not know what's going on up there when we're playing. I don't mean the form and what the technical things are. They don't know or care whether the saxophone has been here eight hundred years or fifty. They don't know whether all the music is memorized or not. They don't know whether we play the same thing every time or if that's what we're trying to do. They have no understanding of what's going on.

A guy said to me in the class I teach—we're talking about the blues form and he said, "Well, was there any indication, were the blues around with the ancient Greeks?" I said, "Let's see if we can't narrow this down to somewhere between the time the boat landed and the latter part of the nineteenth century, that there arose this little twelve-bar thing." I said it's not a vague term that applies to a lot of sorrowful music, it's a particular *form* that's been put together—you know, it *evolved*.

I think perhaps they would not sit there and listen and wait to hear a "tune" if they knew that we were *intending* what we are *attempting*. Are we attempting to make them move or are we attempting to entertain them on the basis of what we intend to do, or they may think we're trying to play better but we just keep making all these clinkers. You wouldn't think that that many people would be that naive, but I have a feeling that when we play for an audience, just a general cross section here, many of them who are listening don't really know what is happening. I'm surprised every time I talk to a group of people about what is jazz and what it means, or what are they playing. They want to know, is it valid, or is it some little thing you sit on a long time and get a horn and fool around with.

KOFSKY: I've heard academics say that you don't have to have any talent to play jazz. You just grab a horn . . .

CARTER: It's only recently that people have come to feel that jazz is a true art form.

BRADFORD: And a lot of them still—

CARTER: Yes, just a few are leaning that way. "Well, maybe there's something to this." There hasn't been—with the exception of a few books —there has not been the in-depth historical research into this to really see.

KOFSKY: Very few.

CARTER: Right. And so there is no history for—

KOFSKY: Perspective?

CARTER: Yes, that people can dig into and come up with something that they can hang onto or make some comparisons with. I think in a few years from now perhaps people will have a better idea of what jazz is all about, what is jazz, and what isn't, what musicians are trying to convey to the audience. I think that it will begin to approach the way people listen to European music, for instance.

BRADFORD: Contrary to what a lot of people believe, in the black community the attitudes towards jazz are not what they would seem.

CARTER: And this has always been true.

BRADFORD: The black parents may say, "Get your horn out and practice, and stop playing all that rag, or playing that jive, and play some *real* music," kind of thing. Which means "I know you can play *that;* that's like jumping off the front porch."

CARTER: This grew out of a whole thing from 'way back with the turn of the century and coming on up through the twenties, when jazz was looked upon negatively by the white community. The black community—

BRADFORD: Reflected a great deal of it.

CARTER: Of course. Trying to be like the white community, it reflected the same disapproval. You'd be surprised in how many black homes that Duke Ellington—"Yeah, I've heard of him—he's a bandleader"—but the music . . . I remember, in fact, one particular occasion when Duke Ellington came to Dallas in 1949 and played at a place that was used for the Ice Capades ordinarily. You'd figure at a thing of that size the entire black community would turn out—about fifty people showed up. Duke left Dallas . . . he would never come back there again. It was almost ten years before he did. Now the black community turned out for jazz at the Philharmonic, which was a music that related itself, I think, to what I call functional music among the black people.

BRADFORD: Like music to dance to and for parties. Like I'm having a party and there are certain records that go with a party. It's Lionel Hampton and it's the Jazz at the Philharmonic kind of thing. If you became sophisticated and really started to listen, you should start to buy Duke Ellington. But it was the rhythm and blues thing, and black people *still* do not think of the creativity that's in that, as related to the jazz thing. It's just "our dance-and-have-fun music." Do you know what I mean? It's thought of, too, as a plaything. In a sense, I guess, perhaps it is—it was born out of functional music, that was played for a purpose, to entertain. It reached a point, I suppose, where people would come and sit down and just listen to it for music's sake. But I think it's still probably related to by the greater number as functional kind of music. That's why only a smaller portion of the black communities were supporting a Charlie Parker. They had a head count which showed that more whites were listening to Charlie Parker than blacks.

KOFSKY: No question about that—there are more whites than blacks. It seems difficult to find the middle of the road between the white community, which, when it listens to serious music is ultraserious and doesn't react at all in an emotional way, and the black community which listens to music mainly, as you say, from a functional standpoint. I've found, in lecturing, that when whites who have no background in jazz try and listen to jazz, they do try to overintensify it, as if to say they have to listen entirely cerebrally.

BRADFORD: It's amazing how you can find a person approaching jazz at one stage in their listening career intellectually, and finally it occurs to them that it is fun.

CARTER: It takes a long time, first of all. You have to go into a thing like this completely with the idea of trying to play the kind of music that you want to play. When I say that, I mean, if we wanted to get into a thing that would give us as much freedom as we could have to play whatever we wanted to play as long as it made some kind of musical sense. You just don't start out with that kind of thing figuring on making a big pile of money right quick. We tried to polish and we tried to perfect it, so it has come along. I have always thought that if what you're doing has some merit—well, you know, it will finally do something. Somebody will hear you or you'll find some way to go.

Pharaoh Sanders
Interview by Jazz & Pop

J & P: You're sort of a mysterious man. A lot of people in the music business and even, I guess, out of the music business—the general audience out there—listening to you and buying your records, really do not know too much about your background. Where were you born, Pharaoh?

PHARAOH: Arkansas, North Little Rock, Arkansas.

J & P: When did you first become interested in music?

PHARAOH: Well, the time that I got in music was at the age of sixteen. Before, my main thing was to be an artist. My first instrument was drums. Drums and clarinet—I liked the clarinet, played it for five years.

J & P: Did you actually study? Did you take lessons from a teacher?

PHARAOH: No. I took it up in school, the school band.

J & P: And I suppose there was an instructor there—

PHARAOH: Right. The instructor played trumpet, so he was one of those what you call jazz musicians—

J & P: Yes. But fifteen years old seems a little late to get into music. Most often, you know, kids are a lot younger when they get into music. What made you—

PHARAOH: Wait that long?

J & P: Well, what made you wait that long and what really excited you? What made you want to get into music at the age of fifteen? What did you hear to make you want to play?

PHARAOH: Well, I went to school, Lincoln Junior High School, and at that time we didn't have what you call, you know, a school band. The only thing they had at that time was just a bugle corps. Drum. Fife. You know, the only time that I could really get into any instrument was when I left junior high.

J & P: What did you do during high school?

PHARAOH: Well, when I got to high school I played in Arkansas—I played with the local musicians.

J & P: What kind of music were you playing then? What were the bands like?

PHARAOH: I was playing what they used to call rhythm and blues. And sometimes I'd get jobs with just my horn and guitar. And sit in with different groups—bands that came in town. Like Bobby Blue Bland. I don't think that he would remember me—you know. That was pretty long ago.

J & P: What was the first heavy jazz you heard?

PHARAOH: You mean like an influence?

J & P: Right.

PHARAOH: Well, down the street from me, there was kind of a restaurant, where you'd go in and buy hamburgers and beer and sit out in the car or go inside and sit down and listen to music. Well, this one record that they had in there was "Hard to Get." It don't know whether you've heard of it or not. The alto on it was pretty heavy.

J & P: Well, what happened after high school, when you were playing with these R and B bands?

PHARAOH: Well, when I finished high school I went to Oakland, California. That was in 1959. And I met some local musicians there.

J & P: Who were some of the fellows you played with out there?

PHARAOH: I played with Ed Kelly. And I played with Robert Porter. And I played with Monte Waters, who is in New York now. Dewey Redmond also, on the Coast.

J & P: What made you go to Oakland?

PHARAOH: Well, I had gotten a scholarship in music and at the time, you know, I just wanted to get out of the South. And I think it was a good time for me to leave anyway.

J & P: That takes us to 1959 or to '60. When did you first hear of Coltrane and when did you first meet him?

PHARAOH: Well, the first time I heard of him—the bands that he was playing with—was in San Francisco.

J & P: When did you leave the West Coast for New York?

PHARAOH: It was 1962 when I came to New York. We came to New York in a car that broke down on us halfway, the axle broke. And we had to beg for money all the way here. Because it was getting cold. That was around Thanksgiving.

J & P: So now, thank God, we've got you to New York. What did you do when you got here?

PHARAOH: Oh, I didn't know anybody. And I didn't have any money. I would hang around clubs and apartments . . .

J & P: You must have been really scuffling—I mean, if you had no money and—

PHARAOH: Well, I had heard of people coming and playing with the better musicians—

J & P: Did you meet Coltrane again? Around that time, or was it later?

PHARAOH: No. It's still that first meeting in San Francisco, and at the time he came around with his mouthpiece—he had trouble fitting a mouthpiece. This is a time that I always remember. John asked me if I would go out and help him find some mouthpieces. At the time I had about twenty-five or thirty mouthpieces, and I couldn't find the sound that I wanted out of the mouthpieces, so we looked together. I still can't find the right mouthpiece. Well, anyway, we went through pawnshops and got out this mouthpiece and that one and left that one and went to another—there were lots of pawnshops and it was taking all day long. And in the meantime, he bought some mouthpieces but I don't think—you know—he really felt right with any of them. One mouthpiece that I had he really liked, so I gave it to him. Later, we somehow got into a conversation about meat, and how come I don't eat meat myself. Then into the spiritual thing. I think a lot about God, and what a man puts into his body, you know. But I think I want to get into the heart of things—if a person was aware of the deeper part of himself, I think we would have a more beautiful world.

J & P: You feel that people should eat natural foods?

PHARAOH: Yes, I do think they should eat natural foods. As John did—this we talked about, too.

J & P: John believed in eating foods that were not treated chemically?

PHARAOH: Right. I think that's good because chemical foods really, they seem to make a person, well, if you're a man, it seems to make you more feminine and I don't know whether it does—[Laughter.] I don't know. Anyway, it seems to take away your natural energy. And I think that's a gift of nature.

J & P: The relationship with John was really sort of a spiritual relationship that probably came together slowly as the months went by, and you were both almost living the same way.

PHARAOH: Yes. You know, I called him a lot and pretty soon he started calling me. He would want to talk about the same things that I would be thinking about. We talked about a music center—if I had some money I would have a center where people could come and hear the music.

J & P: I know that this was a strong desire of John's, too.

PHARAOH: Right.

J & P: Do you think that in the past five or six years, that most of the critics, and even the audience, have been fair? Do you think they have understood your music and the music that John was playing? There were and are so many great musicians. The late Eric Dolphy, Albert Ayler, Marion Brown, and Shepp—all these wonderful people. If you think back, it was sort of difficult to present your kind of music—which has been labeled now black jazz or black art music, both good terms. Actually, to boil the question down, do you think it was difficult in the beginning—and how is it now, in comparison? To get the music heard, and what about the critics? Were they helpful or did they hurt you?

PHARAOH: Well, I think the critics hurt it, you know. I think they seem to be against the music. They wrote wrongly about the music and they didn't even know anything about the musicians. They really hurt a lot of musicians. It was an awful job—to just write about the music and not think about the person playing the music. Sure made a person feel bad. That's the sad part, you know. That's why a lot of people now feel like, in *Down Beat*, most of the critics don't seem to know anything about how a person feels or know anything about why he plays his music. I think this is a dangerous thing for anybody to talk about somebody else this way. It's against the law of creation. I think it's a very very dangerous thing for critics to be paid to talk about you. I think that's what it's all about. Getting paid to try to eliminate a lot of people—artists, talent.

J & P: So you think it's true, that there is no question but that you and Coltrane and a lot of musicians turned everything around from the old conception of what jazz music is supposed to be (and there are these old critics and the old audience who really don't know what the hell is going on) so that their reaction immediately was, "Well we don't understand it, so we don't like it and it's no good."

It seems to me that basically, these are young musicians playing new exciting jazz and the audience that's reacting is a young audience and even the critics who dig the new music are young critics. The old critics, who don't want anything to change, who want the status quo to stay, are the people who really cause all the trouble.

PHARAOH: I feel that if a person wants to play music, you know, he just takes what he has and comes out to play. You know, I always feel that if you have something to say, then play no matter what. If you've got that kind of energy you should play—it's like I say to you, come on out and play.

J & P: Some of the sounds today actually bother old-line critics. The sounds of the different players are new and irritating to many of the old-time listeners.

PHARAOH: It didn't really matter to me because I wanted to play, and wherever I could play, I would try to go and play. But I feel like I am still trying to bring out the best of myself, and I haven't even found the right mouthpiece yet. I don't know what it is, but there is something that keeps me wanting to change the sound and keep going on to new and different sounds and forms of music.

J & P: Do you feel that you are getting to more people now?

PHAROAH: Well, I see more people coming out, you know, coming out to the clubs.

J & P: Well, doesn't that make you feel good?

PHARAOH: Let me put it this way, you know—because I play and work more than ever. I always wanted to be a musician, and play for more people—that's what I really wanted to do. So I seem to be accomplishing this.

J & P: Are you going to be doing any traveling? Will you be getting out into other parts of the country? Are people going to see you in person?

PHARAOH: Yes, we will travel more than ever. We are going to Boston, Texas, Los Angeles, and to Europe. It will be good to see the people.

J & P: Well, with the success of *Tauhid* and now *Karma,* you have a wave of followers all over the world. It's too bad John isn't here to enjoy all of this interest in black music. Also, I might add, to enjoy the chagrin of those old bald-headed and gray-haired critics.

PHARAOH: Oh wow! Right. Thanks.

Elvin Jones: The Rhythmic Energy of Contemporary Drumming by David C. Hunt

Preliminary evaluations of the New Thing indicate that the standards of jazz in the 1960s changed dramatically as a result of a new aesthetic philosophy. The process of acquiring, developing, and knowledgeably utilizing technique in a literal representation of the artist's psyche truly became subordinate to the raw physical act of music creation. For the contemporary drummer, the new emphasis on "action," or released energy, mirrors an enactment of the drummer's own psyche and allows other players and listeners to have a direct and immediately accessible path into the deepest recesses of his creative individuality.

Undisputed as the present major influence in contemporary drumming, Elvin Jones creates a rhythmic excitement which surpasses the efforts of all previous modern drummers. His conception is based on complete independence of all four limbs, but does not depend for its strength on any unnecessary stress being placed on one particular component of the drum set or on the basic pulse of a performance itself. Jones blends his high hat, snare drum, bass drum, ride cymbals, and tom-toms with the improvisations of other players through an enormously complex polyrhythmic energy. The structure of this energy is such that one rhythm pattern may be entwined with other rhythms so that their paths meet, run parallel, separate, and meet again with variations in speed, volume, tonal color, and use of space simultaneously influencing the overall flow of ideas.

LeRoi Jones, a writer dedicated to black art and the social cause of the black man, described the emotional heat of this unique drummer's uninhibited drive in the liner notes for the Impulse album, *Coltrane at Birdland.* Jones wrote:

"The long tag of 'Afro-Blue,' with Elvin thrashing and cursing beneath Trane's line, is unbelievable. Beautiful has nothing to do with it, but it is . . . You feel when this is finished, amidst the crashing cymbals, bombarded tom-toms, and above it all Coltrane's soprano singing like any song you can remember, that it really did not have to end at all, that this music could have gone on and on like the wild pulse of all living."

Jones uses triplets freely in simulating and interweaving various forms of triple meter (3/4, 3/8) and compound duple meter (6/4, 6/8) with the standard 4/4, but seldom marks off any regular beat with his high hat. The accent on the weak beats of each measure (2 and 4 in 4/4 time) disappears entirely, to be replaced by intricate cross-rhythms on the ride cymbal reinforced by familiar snare-drum accents, sometimes so dense as to comprise a separate solo while yet accompanying another player. Jones does register the basic pulse subconsciously, but grafts such a complex series of coordinated rhythms onto it that frequently a secondary tempo is created. The preset metronomic tempo is always very exacting in an Elvin Jones performance; the other players, however, must determine this tempo out of his explosive bursts of polyrhythmic energy.

Although Art Blakey, Philly Joe Jones, and Max Roach are capable of producing an extremely tight-knit rhythmic accompaniment behind a front-line soloist, Elvin Jones's daring looseness and frenzied patterns bring him much closer to other improvisers because of the entwining nature of his conception. He actually converses rhythmically with the soloist he is accompanying. In the eight years that he backed tenor saxophonist John Coltrane, complete empathy was established and Jones literally became a part of his leader's improvisations.

Interviewed by *Down Beat's* Don DeMicheal in the early sixties, Jones spoke at length of his artistic relationship to Coltrane:

"It may sound like a duet or a duel at times, but it's still a support I'm lending him, a complementary thing. It's being done in the same context of the earlier style, only this is just another step forward in the relationship between the rhythm section and the soloist. It's much freer—John realizes he has this close support, and, therefore, he can move further ahead; he can venture out as far as he wants without worrying about getting away from everybody and having the feeling he's out in the middle of a lake by himself."

In the mid-fifties, prior to the artistic synthesis of Elvin Jones and John Coltrane, jazz drumming entered a significant period of transition. The standard techniques of this period, having been advanced by Kenny Clarke and Max Roach in the previous decade, were solidified into a strong blues-rooted music known as Hard Bop. There was both a reaffirmation of, and a reaction against, the highly elaborate military style which utilized the drum set as a snare drum with supporting components (bass drum, tom-toms, and cymbals). Rhythmic accompaniment to front-line soloists took two basic directions in this period:

1. a very loose-flowing conception characterized by a constant rhythmic foundation of coordinated independent fill-ins, uplifting drum set figures, and thunderous roll patterns—Art Blakey, Max Roach, and Art Taylor typified this approach.

2. a razor-sharp, crackling style with aggressive snare-drum punctuations and a clipped, but technically precise and exciting method of phrasing—Jimmy Cobb and Roy Haynes were the leading exponents of this style.

Philly Joe Jones, probably the most influential drummer of the mid-fifties, combined both styles of playing in his masterful conception. Charlie Persip another brilliant soloist of both small-group and big-band persuasion in this period, incorporated many characteristics of the second approach into what was basically a roll-oriented solo conception and established himself as an extremely flexible artist capable of propelling Dizzy Gillespie's big band or Harry "Sweets" Edison's quintet.

With the advent of the New Thing movement, the most daring conceptions of jazz drumming became conscious translations of historically important ideas into structured and unstructured instinctiveness. Technique became inseparable from content or form. Knowing how to play drums out of the exercise book and applying such knowledge to a conceptual command of other drummers' solos and timekeeping characteristics only resulted in a creative superficiality. Profundity in artistic performance demanded complete dedication to the achievement of original content in music, to the almost total exclusion of technical identification with the work of major drummers Art Blakey, Philly Joe Jones, and Max Roach.

The endless changes of direction, rhythmic liberation, and melodic impetus inherent in the fabric of the New Thing gave drummers invaluable freedoms. No longer did they have to repetitiously state the rhythmic pulse of jazz in the traditional sense. The renaissance of Elvin Jones proved that conclusively. His coordinated blanket of sound acted as both a melodic stimulus and a rhythmic launching pad for other improvisers.

Although Jones's newly discovered conceptual and technical freedoms greatly enhanced the emotional and intellectual facets of creating contemporary jazz, there still remained the question of how he could trespass on the improvisatory opportunities given other soloists without seriously interfering with the melodic content of their performances. Melody and rhythm are essentially bound up with each other in the course of a player's improvisation. If a front-line soloist is continually subordinating his own rhythm to Jones's constant barrage, the possibility exists that he will be unable to create a self-satisfying melodic line. Many players possessing less artistic strength than that of tenor saxophonists John Coltrane, Joe Henderson, and Wayne Shorter have already found this to be true.

The contemporary drummer who consistently performs in the combined solo-multiphrasing style frequently loses all feeling for dynamics in the energetic climate of improvisation, with the full volume of the drum set dramatically overpowering other rhythm-section players as well as the front-line soloist. Initially, Elvin Jones experienced this dilemma with frustrating regularity, but the masterful control which he presently displays over every component of his drum kit makes his conception a unique joy rather than a constant annoyance. His swirling current of brush rhythm behind Earl "Fatha" Hines on a recent Contact album (SC-6, *Here Comes Earl "Fatha" Hines*) are ample proof of a mature sensitivity beautifully developed and executed.

Jones deliberately plays and implies rhythms that are the opposite of those inherent in the improvisations of most soloists, but he is attuned to the revolving leadership of collective interplay that is the chief characteristic of contemporary jazz groups and his unfailing ear gives him a decided advantage over other drummers attempting similar artistic goals. As each player improvises, Jones becomes an artistic polarity in relation to them. He stimulates every soloist and is in turn stimulated himself, producing a spiraling emotional interaction in the course of each individual or collective passage. In many instances, a composition becomes so thoroughly infused with the Elvin Jones polyrhythmic energy, it begins to sound as if it is his personal artistic property.

As a drum soloist, Jones exhibits the same kind of uninhibited drive that sparks his rhythmic accompaniment. Bashing pyramids of snare and bass drum patterns are capped by thundering rolls and splashing bursts of cymbal embroidery to heighten an already unbearable emotional energy created out of his percussive support to other players. Jones has recently embraced the philosophy that a solo is a vehicle of personal freedom.

Expressing his feelings to Don DeMichael in a *Down Beat* article entitled "The Sixth Man," Jones said:

"Sometimes I've used accelerandos and decelerandos in my solos. It seems a natural thing to do because it's a *solo*. And a solo can take any form the artist chooses; he can use any form he wants within the framework of the composition. It goes back to getting away from the rigidity that jazz had to face when it was primarily dance music."

Reviewing Jones in his new trio setting, Hubert Saal of *Newsweek* wrote:

"Jones's solos are in fact sonatas for drums, exploring rhythms as other instruments explore melodies. In his composition 'The Long 2/4,' his flabbergasting twenty-minute solo began with the simple 2/4 cadence of a marching band and with punishing speed spiraled upward and outward in increasingly complicated variations on the basic rhythm, building a metrical skyscraper floor by floor until the original tempo seemed lost. But it wasn't. It was conspicuous by its absence, felt rather than heard, the invisible base against which he launched a bewildering barrage of contrapuntal rhythms and even, by some Jonesian sleight of hand, percussive dissonance."

The modern jazz drum solo, despite its acceptance by audiences throughout the world, has never gained much favor with the critical fraternity; even fellow artists tend to hear their own drummer's improvisation in terms of a technical display or "a loosening up of chops." That today's drummer actually relates to the melody and form of the composition he is improvising on in an artistically meaningful way still mystifies those listeners who think of rhythm only as an accompaniment factor or musical propellent. In the mid-sixties, Elvin Jones began successfully to combat this ignorance by elevating the drum solo to the status of a classic production. Today there are few critics or musicians who would not rate his solos as some of the best in contemporary jazz.

Jones's recorded output is prodigious and one need only examine the series of John Coltrane quartet albums on Impulse or recent Blue Note releases under the leadership of tenor saxophonists Joe Henderson and Wayne Shorter to appreciate his genius.

Elvin Jones is *the rhythmic energy* of contemporary drumming. His technique is authentically individual. His conception defies imitation. And should any reader already have felt that Jones plays *impossible* drums, this writer's advice is to study the instrument for ten years and play for fifteen—you'll be even more convinced.

Sunny Murray:
The Continuous Cracking
of Glass
by Robert Levin

*"I work for natural sounds rather than
trying to sound like drums. Sometimes I try
to sound like car motors or the continuous
cracking of glass."*

Sunny Murray

In *Black Music* LeRoi Jones depicts Sunny Murray, the major drum force in the jazz of the sixties, in action:

. . . it is immediate, his body-ness, his physicality in the music. Not just as a drum beater but as a conductor of energies, directing them this way and that way . . . Sunny lunges and floats over the drums and cymbals, striking, near-striking, brushing, missing, caressing all the sound surfaces . . . His rhythmic reorganization makes the drums songful. His accents are from immediate emotional necessity rather than the sometimes hackneyed demands of a prestated meter, in which one cymbal is beat upon coyly in the name of some fashionable soulforce. The drums surprise and hide and are subtle or suddenly thunderous. In some passages Murray has both feet working, straightout, and the drumsticks (which are metal tubes, or knitting needles, even sometimes, wood) are not even visible. The drum "line" swoops, is loud, is soft, and sometimes seems to disappear as well. But it is total drum music Murray makes, not just ear-deafening "ac-companiment" . . . [Sunny] wants "natural" sounds, natural rhythms. The drums as a reactor and manifestor of energies coursing through and pouring out of his body. Rhythm as occurrence. As natural emphasis. You hear him moaning behind his instrument, with his other beautiful instrument. His voice. The sound of feeling. The moan, a ragged body-spasm sound, like some heavy stringed instrument, lifting all the other sounds into prayers.

If concentration camps for blacks are, indeed, a forthcoming reality in this country, the case for them will no doubt be clinched in reaction to what that passage observes.

I.e., "The sound of feeling."

The most pernicious effect of four hundred years of oppression and exploitation of the black man in America (to be sure, the principle objective of the "program") was his imprisonment, in a paralyzing ambivalence. Those forces which externally operated to limit the size and scope of his reality and his possibilities came, through centuries of conditioning, to have their *internal* counterpart, to inhabit his psyche. If a part of the black man could recognize that he was at least as worthy of existence as the white man who despised him, he was also half-convinced that he deserved to be despised, and the cruel tensions of that ambivalence withered his best revolutionary impulses and rendered him incapable of significantly altering his condition. He could not really believe enough in his *right* to alter it.

The dynamism behind both black nationalism and the aesthetics of the new jazz (the quest for a revolution of *sensibility* and the achievement of spiritual consciousness which these correlative phenomena embody in their best manifestations) has been a passion for life (not just survival) unleashed in the inevitable explosion of that ambivalence. And it is this passion generated by the black man's liberation from uncertainty regarding the worthiness of his identity, not, per se, the revolutionary sentiments and rhetoric of black leaders or the rejection of certain traditional conventions by new jazz players, which most upsets the powers that be. For passion, unprogrammable by the computer, is the only real enemy of the technological society, the only force that can give real motion to ideas and the mechanisms of genuine change; i.e., the only energy that can break ideas past the ambuscades of assimilation, co-optation, and control, and open, expand, and restructure the narrow and aberrated emotional orders in which the powers that be are trapped and would keep the rest of us trapped. (John Cage, for example, is as "advanced" a musician as Cecil Taylor, but because his music is totally cerebral, he disturbs nobody's sleep. All head, he can do no better than describe—albeit ingeniously—our condition; he cannot transcend it.)

Thus in defense of a pathological emotional order, and in a complex of subtle and blatant ways—in the name of reason or sanity, maturity, health, law and order, etc., America has been commited to the suppression, the dispersal, enervation, and neutralization of passion. Passion will, in whatever form it may take, create jailers (social workers, senators, clergymen, psychiatrists . . . reactionary jazz critics).

It is very apparent, sitting in an audience at a new jazz performance, that the particular anxiety which a Sunny Murray, a Cecil Taylor, an Archie Shepp, or an Albert Ayler provokes in many people is only by degrees different from that which a riot will stir in them—the same circuits are disrupted. When the destruction of property occurs in a riot, it isn't the potential collapse of his economic position, as such, that distresses the businessman, but the destruction of the boundary markers of his uptight emotional order which that property represents. The "continuous cracking of glass" down 125th Street would set all the businessmen free, too.

Sunny Murray incisively verbalizes aspects of the new music, and some of its profound *extra*musical implications and ramifications:

"In a way what this whole thing is about—and dig the revolutionary enormity of this—is that now a cat plays to find out what a horn sounds like *before* studying it! It's also about getting back to natural, everyday sounds, sounds which are very different today than they were when I was a kid and when bebop was what was happening. A lot of times I sit very still and quiet in my crib and try to listen to every sound that happens within one second—which is a lot of sound to hear at once. I try to condition myself to be able to hear all of them. Society tries not to hear natural sounds—they disrupt the hearing of the people, they aren't 'listenable.' But to disturb people—at least what *they* mean by disturb—that's the whole point. That's why we have to bring natural sounds up front again. Like in a hospital: if some avant-garde jazz musicians played outside a hospital they'd say they were going to kill the patients or make them sicker because the patients weren't in tune to that sound. But maybe it was them working so hard not to hear natural sounds that contributed to putting them as patients in the hospital in the first place. And maybe the sounds we make could touch and unloose something in those patients and make them want to live again. You see the intensity of this music can really change things; the elements we live in, the air and the water.

"Our ears play a greater role in this music than our minds do. Because of our inhibitions our music has to heard over and over until the sensitivity in the listener's ear is finally broken through to so that it can respond to natural sounds. For a while this music may put you into a bag that you don't understand because it's your unconscious mind that's digging it and not your conscious mind, which is trying to cut it off. But once you're into this music you'll find that you're much more aware and able to cope with the world around you. Like, children who haven't had time yet to develop a wall against it, they *love* the new music, they go crazy over it like they go crazy over James Brown. When they hear like 'progressive' jazz they cut it off. They can't dig that. Look how lucky they are—the kind of conditioning they're getting. I didn't have that conditioning when I was a child. This opens up their whole life. I can understand why kids listen to rock and roll. They listen to their parents arguing—their pop sitting up all day looking at TV, or their mom walking around the house looking like a polar bear. R & R is a complete breakaway for them, it's freedom. That's why R & R is supported by them. Of course, *some* older people *do* hear it. Don Byas told me when he heard Albert Ayler play that he always wanted to play that way since he was a boy. There was something in his mind like that all the time. He didn't say, man, that's crazy shit you're playing and that's not what's happening. All he thought was here's a cat who's come along and who's decided to play his horn the way he wants to play it. And he was full of admiration. Dig it—if Bird had let himself really go, twenty-five years ago, we'd be past all the hostility and really out there by now. Of course, R & R and avant-garde jazz is still not supported by a certain area. A certain area considers it a disaster. They wouldn't have this music at the White House. If they did, they would all think they were being attacked. All of a sudden an R & R or an avant-garde jazz musician jumps and goes into his thing, and these people would run and hide under tables because all their guilt would scare hell out of them. Now if Lawrence

John Coltrane

Photo by Irv Glaser/Courtesy Flying Dutchman Productions

John Carter and Bobby Bradford

John Coltrane

Photo by Katsuji

Pharaoh Sanders

Cecil Taylor

Elvin Jones

Sunny Murray

Horace Tapscott

Oliver Nelson

Photo by Charles Stewart

Gary Bartz

Archie Shepp

Photo by Charles Shabacon

Ornette Coleman

Leon Thomas

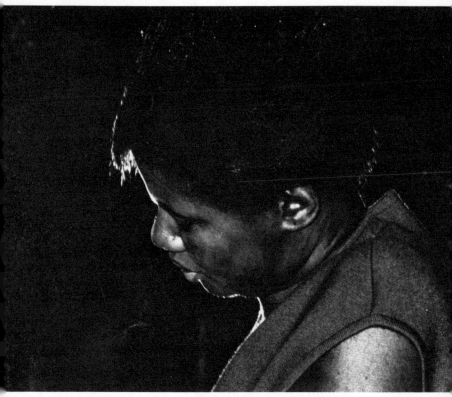

Alice Coltrane

Welk plays there—doo-pee-doo—oh, they cool now, man. The submission in the music tells them that the people is submissioned. But if the musician is acting like a rock or an avant-garde jazz musician does, then what are the people acting like? Like when they had the March on Washington, the one the government approved of [the 1963 civil-rights march], what did they have? At best they had *hip* doo-pee-doo music.

"Rock and avant-garde jazz are really contributing to the downfall of a lot of bullshit in this country."

Sunny first came to New York as a bebop drummer—a malcontent bebop drummer. He could not find his originality within what was then the still prevailing system. In 1959 he encountered Cecil Taylor.

"I was at a little place in the West Village called the Café Roue. I came in one night with a cat named Wade who had just bought a bass yesterday. Cecil came in a few minutes later and sat in a corner with his collar up over his head. All the dudes immediately started packing up and when I asked them why they said, 'You don't know Cecil Taylor. They way he plays, can't *no*body get together with him.' Well, you know, I've always admired a cat that stood out in a crowd because it meant he was very . . . very useful! He was a necessity. He wasn't one to shun, he was one to dig. And I thought, if you pack up when a man comes in to play then he must be *something*. Let some more come in that make you pack up and I'll be around some really good musicians. It was like when I was hanging out on the corner with the guys in Philadelphia. If a cat would come up who the other cats didn't like I'd want to know why, and if they gave me some sick-assed reason I'd say to the cat who'd come up, 'Let's *you* and *me* split,' and I'd leave *them* there. So I said, 'Listen man, I'm going to play with him,' and they said, 'Go ahead, we will listen.' So I went over to Cecil and introduced myself and said, 'I would like to play with you. I don't really play that good, but I would like to play with you.' And he said, 'Do you know how I play?' And I said, 'No." He said, 'Are you *sure* you want to play with me?' I said, "Yeah.' He took off his coat and everybody got all tense and he went to the piano and started playing.

"Well, you know, in '59 it was a little different. I said to myself, damn, he sure *is* into something else, and I struggled along. But I played a whole three tunes. Wade played too, even though he couldn't really play and Cecil said, 'That's all right, let him do it if he wants.' Cecil laughed. He had fun. A couple of times I didn't know what to do and I just stopped and Cecil turned around and said, 'No, keep going, don't stop.' Other drummers had played with him of course, but they had played something conventional like *tanka-ting*. But I decided not to play that way. I was playing on one. Like Elvin was playing on one in Detroit, but I didn't know about him. I thought it was hip to play on one. Bass players would always say, 'Oh motherfucker, you keep turning the beat around.' So a lot of cats didn't like me, though some cats did.

"I went back to play with the beboppers after that night and they all started laughing and kept saying, 'Hey, Sunny played with Cecil,' and making a big joke out of it. And I was thinking, who *is* Cecil? Who the devil *is* this cat I played with? And I looked for Cecil, man, for days, every day. I thought, I ain't heard nobody play like that and I'm gonna make sure that I can play with him again 'cause I knew he had enjoyed my playing and it wasn't like I was bugging his nerves.

"Finally I found Cecil at the old Cedar Bar. He helped me get a loft on Dey Street in a building where he was living. After I moved in I knocked on his door. There was no answer, but as it happened we had the same set of keys so I opened the door and set my drums up and he was lying in bed looking at me. I said, 'You don't mind, do you?' And he said, 'Uh um.' And I set 'em up. But I was too nervous to start playing with the cat in bed. It took me about three weeks to decide, well I'm gonna play anyway. I've got to practice and my drums is over there now, and he said, 'OK.' So I played, but he wouldn't get out of bed. Matter of fact, he never let nobody see him out of the bed and his windows was open up about twelve inches and I'd be trying to talk to him and shivering and finally I said, 'I can't talk to you like this. Can I please close your windows?' And he said, 'OK.' I'd been practicing there with a big coat on and I was getting tired of it. Then one day Cecil finally got up to play with me. He got up to play on his old beat-up upright piano and said, 'I want you to play something like you never played before.' I said, 'What do you mean, like a drum solo?' And I started to play a drum solo and Cecil said, 'No, -stop. Just let yourself play.' So I thought, let myself play? That's kind of weird. But I guess I've got that kind of mind, being a Virgo, so I just let myself play. I wasn't really aware that he was leading me into a new musical system until about 1962."

Sunny's extraordinary talent, intelligence, and wit have survived thirty-two years in America. Born in southeastern Oklahoma of black slave and American Indian ancestry, he has withstood the death of the uncle who took care of him as a child and who was refused treatment at an Oklahoma City hospital because he was black; an adolescence in the bestial streets of slum Philadelphia (rats and pigs everywhere); the OD death of the stepbrother who introduced him to music; two years in a Pennsylvania reformatory; an industrial accident in which a couple of fingers were torn away; countless mean jobs (his music being persistently unnegotiable) as a building superintendent, car washer, etc. Sunny has gone through all that and more, but each time you hear him (usually on a borrowed set of drums), his playing is even stronger, even more focused, vibrant, spiritually tuned.

In addition to being a musician and composer of exceptional endowments, Sunny, like Taylor, his mentor, can claim a comprehension of the scene, and his own position in relation to it, that is remarkably keen. And this is what has saved him. He recognizes the jeopardy in which his effusive vitality and audacious aesthetic puts him, and is acutely aware of the multifarious forms of ambush. He has learned how to keep himself alive and growing in an environment that is murderously hostile to such pursuit.

"What about the H-Bomb?" a friend asked him a couple of years ago. And he could answer, "Ah, I don't really believe they have one. They just tell us they do to keep us in line."

Sunny is working hard at giving real substance to the notion of the emancipated slave.

"You have to dig what happened to other black innovators. Like Bird. Bird didn't even know what he was swept into. All he knew was that he was playing. If he had known what was happening around him he would still be here as far as I'm concerned. He would have figured some way how to realize who he was and not let them destroy him. Though Trane's outlook became more and more beautiful, I think he realized a little too late who he was. He spent half his life supporting the Mafia. The crucial thing you've got to understand is who you are and work on it and preserve it. Then you're not going to die from no strange shit. Like what happened to Eric Dolphy. He didn't look at what was happening around him. He didn't realize how dangerous them people around him were. The powers want to manipulate a young cat. The position they've got Shepp in he'll really be uptight in above five years—his energy could possibly beat them . . . I don't think Albert has found a way. Cecil has, but we can't all be Cecil.

"The business world says that the only way you can make it is to try and play like someone else. They create competition and enemies. They also try to put out the illusion—in order to try and stop you from really getting anywhere—that an artist can never be satisfied. But I don't believe that. I believe that I can do something musically, satisfy myself, and go on. A beboper's credo is like, no, man, if you're really a musician then you can't never be satisfied. Like Pharaoh and Charles Lloyd. Now, if them two dudes ain't satisfied that they can play like Trane by now then they should quit music, man. Pharaoh played the last squeak with him and Charles has played all the way up to '67. They should start playing some other shit. But they're not, they're saying, well now, man, I'm still trying to get it. That same old-fashioned ideology that they're not satisfied. I can't use it. If I told myself that I'd never done nothing really proper or correct I'd be going home to play some shit that's been out of style for twenty years. I'm even satisfied with what I played the last time I played. I want to play something else now. I bet if we are sitting around with some beboppers right now they'd put me down. Oh, you ain't no musician, Jim, if you think you can be satisfied. Why should I let them brainwash me? The only way you can really be creative is to finish with something—decide that it is finished. I want to have the kind of mind that lets me go on to another thing. Like a scientist. OK, we cured this disease. Bang! Let's go on. Like Louis Pasteur. They ain't fucked with the milk since then, except maybe diluted it a little bit. And that's a revelation to the people who come and hear this music. They know they can come and hear something that constantly moves and changes.

"Another destructive thing the business world does is not letting a musician find out who he is. They take him and *tell* him who he is. They disrupt groups by picking players out, ignoring the unity of groups and destroying that unity. They disrupt the development of individual players that way. They say to a cat, you're a heavy cat, the heaviest cat in the spirit world. And they sap his energy. So out of twenty bands you get three that are really good. And the commercial world uses this as evidence that avant-garde jazz is shit. They take a band that everybody who knows knows isn't together, and they say, look at this, this is an example of avant-garde. They don't want to differentiate between them and an artist like Cecil Taylor. They don't want to hear the difference. So they feed the cats that can't play and starve out the cats who can. Like if you watch a movie today you can hear avant-garde music, but you hear a poor imitation of it. Studio musicians imitating an interesting and important music, rather than genuine sound-effecting musicians. The guys who have gotten out front should tell the truth about this. You see the system offers large sellouts to those they think will *deteriorate by having* and ignores those they think will deteriorate by *not having*. It's two ways of getting the same safe result—nothing.

"The business world wants everybody to agree to the same shit. The few innovators who insist on creativity *along* with filling their grocery bag are the ones who will establish that the music will last.

"There are still too few people who can, or want to understand why this music is and what it contributes. When they listen to a Charles Lloyd record, for instance, they can't see why this music has to exist. Like, aren't the Negroes happy. If a man makes money that way, then let him contribute to the really creative musicians who play what they really believe in, so that those musicians don't have to scuffle so much. Scuffling and learning diplomacy tends to make you concentrate more on getting the job than on the job itself. It's very dangerous. You can concentrate so much on getting the job that you get to the gig with nothing left to play. And that's exactly what they want to have happen."

Sunny played with some top-level bop musicians like Jackie McLean and Rocky Boyd, before working and recording with Cecil Taylor for several years. He has also, beside recording with a number of other leaders, notably Archie Shepp and Albert Ayler, made three albums of his own: *Psychology of Drums* (Jihad), *Spiritual Truth* (ESP), and *Sunny's Time Now* (Debut). For a period he was coleader (with Ayler) of a group that included Don Cherry and Gary Peacock, and he has worked with many of his own units. None of these ventures provided remuneration sufficient to raise Sunny's annual income above the poverty line. At the time we spoke, however, his circumstances seemed about to improve. He was beginning a series of recording sessions for Columbia, his first record date as a leader for a major label. The album was to consist entirely of his own compositions. Alan Silva, Dewey Redman, Chris Capers, Dave Burrell, Arthur Jones, Sonny Simmons, and Cliff Thornton were among the players he was using.

The Columbia album, called *Spiritual Infinity* (early reports promised stunning music), could serve to ease Sunny's perpetually bleak financial situation and afford him the opportunity, for the first time in his career, of concentrating totally upon his work. If that happens . . . well, it is impossible to speculate about what a talent and energy of the proportions which Murray commands, freed of serious money problems, could reach.*

"So many people believe that to be avant-garde is to furiously beat the drum set as fast and hard as you can, which isn't so. There are hundreds of different percussion systems that don't include beats and beating so furiously. There are 'classical' composers who use percussion in different ways. Cage, Boulez, Stockhausen, Varèse . . . they show me that natural sounds can be tabulated, which I want to do. They have a system for writing down the sound of breaking glass, tearing up your crib—systems and symbols for all that. Three musicians can sit around and play everyday sounds off a chart. I've been trying to get away from beats. It's very hard. But something comes to me and tells me there are other ways. Most avant-garde horn players and lightweight piano players relate to the beat on the drums, which only brings them to one understanding. But it's about understanding the meaning of acoustics—how not to relate to beats so much because beats is just a hereditary force that has followed us all these years.

"Like, to get away from beats is to get away from poverty.

"You see, there's so much to do. Art is the medium to reach John J. Layman, to explain to him what this thing he's hung up in called the world is about, and to give him a format and outline. If he doesn't listen, or if obstacles are set up to stop him from listening, there's just gonna be more destruction. When you stop and look at some of the older cats and see what happened to them, then you know this music and the attitudes that go with it have *got* to be right. Like Diz—he's a shell of a man now. I saw him on TV the other night. He can't even smile anymore. And so many of the bebop drummers have been destroyed by the businessman. I don't want to follow the course of any bebop drummers. The best thing I can do for the bebop drummer is liberate him.

"I thought some time ago it would be impossible for me to continue playing this way—I thought it was just gonna disappear from me like the way it came. But it hasn't and now I don't think it ever will. I thought it was something unnatural that I was playing and I was very disturbed. I used to listen to tapes of myself and wonder if I was going crazy. One of the things that kept me cool was that I had a few 'crazy' friends like C. T. and Henry Grimes.

"Now I feel like as I'm getting older I'm getting closer to beauty. To me it's about being knocked out of your head by hearing your *own* shit. This is what I think is beautiful. When you get to this point then you know you're taking care of business.

"America is trying to destroy us and this music. I think of all the horizons that we haven't even touched and sometimes when I look at how the avant-garde musician has suffered I think, damn, if we haven't

* *Spiritual Infinity*, recorded in early 1969, was never released.

touched all those areas by now, then the way the system has been crushing us we aren't going to be around to get to them. There are a lot of avant-garde drummers around, but the drum set is still largely unexplored.

"But then I think America won't be able to destroy us. We *will* be around—we're too strong. Anybody who's trying to hold this music back is fighting a losing battle because you can't hold something back that's so natural. Now I feel like an old man grown wise by so much destruction, and almost destruction, of something we need. I feel I have to live. And if we are ever going to solve our problems, then this music has to live."

Today's Jazz Artist:
His Communication and
Our Technological Age
by David C. Hunt

It is an undeniable fact that our lives presently lean toward a position nearing total influence by technological development. We seem to have very little time or consideration for the profound questions of human existence as reflected in the spiritual values of various art forms. That today's jazz artist has successfully survived two self-imposed redefinitions of his craft, bop and the New Thing, in the face of such a dehumanization process is in itself a monumental tribute to his physical and mental stamina. Jazz is certainly not dead, but the individual artist is steadily experiencing the disaster of seeing his position in American society uprooted even further from the already dubious status he has attained since the thirties.

Before examining the juxtaposition of jazz and the jazz artist to technology and the scientific philosophy, let's define our technological age and find out what it is, how it has influenced the values of the people that live in it, and whether it is really attempting to answer the profound questions of human existence.

In its original definition, "technics" covered thought-out procedures and actions yielding the achievement of results identifiable with skills. Most skilled activities were based on a general framework of rules which could serve as a further guide when passed on to others. Technics now applies to this framework as a greatly advanced procedure for the production of goods, tools, and tool-producing machines.

In the first half of the twentieth century, technology began to exploit nature on behalf of man's needs. The advanced procedures of production and their effective application to industry brought about rapid economic changes.

The twentieth century presently mirrors the dominance of technology in human life. We have reduced feats of air, distance, comfort, and destruction to mere insignificance by the release of the power energy of the atom. As human beings, we wonder if we are any longer competition for, or masters of, the mechanical and technical advances we have created. It *should* be difficult for us to remain impersonal viewers as we visualize the control of our lives shifting to a completely automated process, but our unquestioned embrace of science and the scientific philosophy would seem to indicate that we will submit willingly to this slavery.

It is for this reason, perhaps more than any other, that the contemporary jazz artist is a valuable spokesman. Philosophically, he has the beautiful capacity, through a musical instrument, to dramatize the human condition. His artistic talking, shouting, singing, moaning, and crying serve to awaken us to the artificial living patterns of our society—the slightness of understanding, the easy acceptance—all that reeks of sterility.

Consider, for a moment, science and the scientific philosophy in protective coatings of logic and verifiability. Protection is guaranteed by refraining from allowing problems that cannot be proved logically to appear before us. Science assures us that philosophy is to be limited to results of abstraction that are subjected to logical analysis for verification. This process would enable only those possessing the exacting qualifications of engineers, mathematicians, and scientists to experience the richest kind of knowledge and communication. Must we continue to submit to those who maintain that knowledge is only valid when perceptible by verification?

Although art and science approach truth through different languages, verifiability is thought to be a part of artistic creation regardless of its form. The expressive quality of art is not primarily the verifiable aspect, although certainly the complete spectrum of emotions is symbolically utilized by the artist. The very fact of being constitutes a strong case for verifiability, and jazz is certainly a form which focuses exclusively on this reality.

Nevertheless, the creative artist has always been under constant fire with the accusation that his form does not produce verifiable truths. Scientists charge that the spontaneous desire for self-realization and the basic creative drive in no way serve truth.

In defense of the creative artist, it must be emphasized that his activity is philosophical and has meaning that can symbolize the most profound spiritual problems of mankind. He approaches modern philosophy through a unique kind of transcendence. In stretching beyond the concreteness of observable matter, he brings into focus an independent conception leading to truth. The message constructed by the artist has philosophical value for himself and his audience. As a result, he combines expression and communication in a single purpose.

The late John Coltrane is the perfect example of a jazz artist who has achieved worldwide prominence through a deep spiritual communication. Truth in the arts demands an intense involvement in life to find aesthetic choices in line with the individual kind of depth in the artist's work. Coltrane's life took on a special significance as he explored most of life's possibilities and immersed himself in the most defined depths of human activity. His resulting acts of creation became focal points of truth in the lives of other human beings.

While the growth patterns of mass production, corporate wealth, and technology have had a decided influence upon the thinking habits of the general public, the jazz artist's own development has also aroused strong feelings, mostly antagonistic, among various segments of the population. In the first redefinition of structure, the revolutionary bop artist embraced rhythms that were too subtle and intricate to dance to. Melody became a fast cascade of notes that had very little impact on the memory of listeners except to startle them and turn them away from any possible acceptance of the virtues of improvisation. Ironically enough, with the advent of bop and musical abstractionism, the music matured and came of age as an art form. For, despite breaking with its own conventions and creating new ones, jazz *remained* a mode of expression and communication based on swing, standard tunes, and the blues.

The second redefinition of jazz, or New Thing, dealt with the alteration of the basic structure and form of the music. Many emotions which weren't expressible in linguistic terms immediately took shape through the contemporary jazz artist's preoccupation with spontaneous feelings and whims. Although preconceived structures were discarded in favor of fresh settings, this was small consolation to ears vainly searching for a recognizable melody or harmony, or a repetitious rhythmic pattern.

The jazz artist of today is an emotional reflector of our society through his musical form of symbolic expression. His major role is to keep the spiritual essence ever before the masses. It is sad, indeed, that our present system of education doesn't prepare us to appreciate his contributions and heed his messages.

By his insistence that technical domination preclude all spiritual considerations, man's inhumanity to himself has increased year after year. The implications of such a catastrophe unaltered in the next 100 years are overwhelming. The possibility of man ultimately making a methodical transformation into a useless entity is real. If, through technological development, science schedules the mechanical substitute for our spiritual activity, man's personal worth to himself and to others will first diminish and then become nonexistent.

The alternative to degenerate man as a slave in a world of central control is a rebirth of man as a spiritual animal. Recognition of today's jazz artist and his continual focus on the human approach to universal truths will aid in that rebirth.

Oliver Nelson's African Tour
Interview by Pauline Rivelli

(The Oliver Nelson septet left the United States for Africa on a State Department tour March 3, 1969. They returned May 1. The septet consisted of Nelson, soprano sax; Stan Gilbert, bass; Bob Morin, drums; Ernie Watts, baritone sax; John Klemmer, tenor sax; Frank Strozier, alto sax; and Freddie Hill, trumpet.

The following interview took place June 2, 1969, while Oliver was in New York City negotiating with Sam Goldwyn, Jr., to write the film score for *Cotton Comes to Harlem*.)

PAULINE: *Jazz & Pop* readers are familiar with the name Oliver Nelson. We have run several articles about you since we've been publishing, and readers are well aware of your victories as arranger and composer in our various critics and readers polls. So let's get right to the moment and talk about your State Department tour in Africa. Generally, how did audiences react to you and your music?

OLIVER: Generally, the audiences came as sort of a surprise, because we were told, first of all, that we wouldn't be able to reach the Africans because we obviously had never reached any Americans. The State Department, being generally what a State Department is, said the music would not be accepted, it was too sophisticated even for an American audience. That's the general statement that was made concerning the music in Washington, D.C., at Charlie Byrd's, and at some point I was advised to change the programming to accommodate what the Africans really wanted to hear, and they said, "Play a little high-life music," which is alien to American culture, and, "Try to get your white drummer to really get some solos together so he can beat up all his drums, because, of course, the drum is a thing with the Africans."

Now, I listened to all of that and properly decided to forget all about it, and I decided that when we went to Africa we would play the music that we play. The surprising thing is that the Africans responded to the music from an emotional point of view, not intellectually. And I can say, now that the tour is over, that the State Department has said that it was so successful that they are projecting a tour in 1970 of Eastern Europe, if we can work out the details of the trip.

So, generally, African audiences responded differently from what we thought. Which is the students, after a performance, would rush up and almost knock all the horns off the bandstand.

We had Africans that you meet, people who run the government in these countries, they responded by having pictures taken with us. The Russians and the Red Chinese are very, very entrenched in Africa, in Mali and in Guinea. So our trip was really a musical presentation, but somehow we got involved in politics whether we liked it or not.

PAULINE: In what way, Oliver?

OLIVER: Well, we ended up defending the American way of life, whatever it is that we have here in this country, whatever the problems are that don't seem to be so great when you are in a country where poverty is a way of life.

PAULINE: Getting back to the music, you mentioned in a recent phone call from the Coast that African music has rhythm but no melody. Will you elucidate?

OLIVER: Well, African music has always been rhythmic. It has always been functional, also. They have what you would call a ritual, in places like Upper Volta; this ritual is enacted, oh, I don't know, once every two weeks and the music that accompanies this is usually music for dancing —a processional, or something where the music plays a functional role.

Now, Africans don't have harmony as we know it. They don't hear music vertically, like we do, in the case of, say, Mozart. They do achieve harmony because several players will be playing something completely different from each other: four players, each playing a different part. They get harmony this way, and you get it as a direct result of the counterpoint, you know. Linear fashion. So harmony doesn't exist as we know it, but rhythmically, the African music is intact; now you see, the music is alien. Most of the music I heard in Africa was alien. It was either completely European-influenced, or harmonically organized. The very fact that the drums are still intact indicates that there has been some resistance on the part of the Africans, maybe unconscious, for the drums have always remained intact, even though the melody sounds like Hymn Number 99. The African hasn't developed his own thing. The African is very busy trying to become as Western as possible because to think Western means to have a car, electricity, a job, to take a vacation, to go to France. And when he sings, he is singing a song about a specific thing, like I remember one story, it was in Upper Volta, and the story was about this girl who came to live with him and she came in and ate up all the food and once the food was gone, she left.

Well, that's functional music. Very functional. It's not, you know, a melody that the guy just wrote down. It's probably been handed down for a long, long time. The very fact that Africa has produced no significant jazz musicians makes me wonder. This is very strange, because in eight French-speaking countries in West Africa, eight major cities, with a population sometimes a million—two hundred thousand would be the smallest—we would invite all the major musicians in all these cities, with an invitation from the U.S. Embassy, United States Information Service, to tell these people that we want an exchange of cultures. And, they said, "Well, okay, let's conduct workshops where we would have all the musicians together." Well, we found when they tried to play the American blues form, the twelve-bar, they didn't know when to change from the

I chord to the IV chord. And I couldn't understand it because all the faces were black, and I said, "Well, you know, if they have black faces, then why the hell can't they play the blues?" That confused me, because then it occurred to me because maybe they can't play the blues because they don't understand the emotional experience connected with whatever it was that happened in this country. My expression at that point was, "Thank God for slavery, because if we hadn't had slavery, we wouldn't have had the music." This brings up another point, too, and I wonder about it because, of course, the government is very concerned about what I have to say, now that I am back.

But when you have a country, any country in West Africa, that has only one radio and only one newspaper, and then the music that you hear on the radio is always slanted toward popular music, you wonder how can there ever be a social revolution when everybody is dancing in the street, and then you look around and you see that everybody is completely poor, nobody has anything.

And I wonder if this means that if you have a society that has absolutely nothing, do you keep them happy by giving them what they think they want, and that is music that they can dance to, not music that would cause them to even think for a minute of social change?

You see, everything grows in Africa. That is one of the things that amazes most people. A person doesn't have to have a job in order to survive there because they have mango trees and all they have to do is reach up and knock it off. They have bananas, the rivers are full of fish. You see, all these things have a direct bearing on everything that's happening in Africa, and I say myself, if you turn on the radio and all you hear is popular music and political speeches, you know, saying that we have a great president and look what he is doing and all the rest. James Brown is very important in Africa, and Otis Redding. But why are they important? This is what I am saying, if the government controls the radio, then they feed the people what they want them to have in terms of culture, and what social change does happen is happening on a very basic level.

For instance, midwifery—they are trying to keep as many children as possible from dying at birth. But we're talking about something very basic now. We are talking about life in its beginning, and if that is a major problem in Africa and if measles is a problem in Africa and smallpox is a problem there and if the life expectancy is up to thirty-five now, you know, what we are talking about? We are talking about a continent that is very hostile in many ways.

In the desert areas the temperature sometimes exceeds 120 degrees, with no humidity. You go out and because you're thinking you're black and can take it you go out and fall right in the middle of the street. Absolutely—it's happened to me. I thought I could stand it because I have a black face. But they called me a *matisse,* which means a person of mixed blood.

PAULINE: Going back to what you said before: our ghettos do not have mango trees and streams full of fish, and music, although it is a salvation in some cases, does not pay the rent. And then, on the other hand, where we're pushing black history as part of our academic curriculum and what have you, where do you see the salvation for the American blacks?

OLIVER: Well, this is one thing that I guess I feel very strongly about because the whole trip in Africa—can I name the countries?

PAULINE: Please.

OLIVER: Cameroon, East and West Cameroon, which is a coastal area. The Ivory Coast. Abidjan—we had a stop in Dahomey, where a great number of slaves came from. Central African Republic, which was Bongi, capital city, on the Ubangi River and I have something to say about that, too. And then Republic of Chad, Republic of Niger, the Republic of Upper Volta, the Republic of Gambia, and the Republic of Senegal, and I must have left something out.

We were even in Nigeria for a very short time, long enough to see how a British or an English-speaking country reacts to a situation which was a hundred and some miles away, Biafra. When we were there, the planes were coming over, the bombers, the fighter planes, and there were helicopters, soldiers with guns, and we felt like we were in a military situation—you know, "Where is your identity card?" The whole thing.

And a man did come over and ask us something but the minute we started to speak, he knew we were not Nigerians. And it was explained to us—one guy who had courage, I would say, asked, "Well, why are you doing this horrible thing in Biafra, all the children starving?" and the guy made it very clear. He said, "How would you have it if, in your country, Detroit decided it wanted to move out of the United States because it discovered gold and platinum, titanium, or anything else?" He said, "We cannot have a runaway province in our own country and we don't have to fire a shot. We simply will work it out, you know, we *want* to work it out. And the Red Cross and the American government interfere, they don't understand our ways." And he is saying, first of all, that it is perfectly logical to starve your enemy to death, no matter if they're women, children, or what, because it's a sensible way. It's a way that works. If you don't understand it, then you really don't understand African ways.

And, of course, we couldn't understand it; you've seen the pictures and everything else, so you know. But what he was saying is that they cannot have a runaway province within their own boundaries. And they achieve results any way they can. We can't begin to think of this. To recap: whatever it is that Africa is, and the reasons why I wanted to go— I'll see if I can make it clear now, the differences. Now, first of all, West Africa is essentially French-speaking, and East Africa is English-speaking, also Portuguese—a lot of people have colonized Africa; what you see, when you go there, is a continent which has been colonized, never enslaved.

Slavery was a big thing, for instance in Bongi, Central African Republic, right on the Ubangi River. I saw a photograph of a Ubangi woman —one of the two or three remaining women from the Ubangi tribe with the wooden blocks in their mouths; you know a lot of people have the notion that this was done because it was considered a beautification thing. But it was really intended to discourage the Arabs from taking the women and selling them as slaves. So what they did was put the blocks into the women's mouths and disfigure them any way they could. Now that slavery no longer exists in this part of Africa, there is no longer the need to disfigure the women, because the slave trade has stopped.

I am saying, you understand now the necessity for the Ubangi tribe to preserve their tribe by disfiguring—and Americans can't begin to understand the reasons why.

Whatever revolution it takes will have to happen on such a basic level. Wigs are being worn now in Africa. Kids want to play electric guitars and not play traditional music. People want to live in the city and don't want to live in the villages anymore. Whatever the social and revolutionary change in Africa, it will take quite a long time, as opposed to the kind of social and revolutionary change that we have here.

So Africa has simply not produced any music other than traditional that can be considered even close to American jazz in any kind of way.

PAULINE: Or American pop, for the matter?

OLIVER: Well, they get pop music from France and West Africa. It's almost like this—if you want to hear the news in Africa and you happen to have a shortwave radio, like I have, you get news slanted to make the Americans look good from Voice of America and you get the news that is slightly tainted in some way from BBC, which is British Broadcasting Company.

And if you really want to hear what happened in Chicago during the riots, then you listen to local radio which, in a sense, tries to put the country down, for whatever reason. So the African, in a sense, is concerned about the movement here in this country. A couple of African students asked, "What was Chicago really like?" They want to know. So it's not that there is no exchange, because there is. We felt very warm with the African people. Musically, you shake another musician's hand, even if he can't play the blues, you know, you can feel something.

PAULINE: Well, the music was basically the bond. Getting back to the American way of life you mentioned earlier, that was criticized by Africans, what was the major American way of life that was criticized?

OLIVER: Well, let's face it, we live in a country where everybody is basically a hypocrite, that's all. You know, well, for instance, Los Angeles, they would prefer Mayor Sam before they will put in somebody about whom there is a reasonable chance that maybe he could have been a good man. But this is what exists in this country and this is what they see, they say, "Well, how do you explain the fact that Mayor Lindsay who is white can't get anything done in New York?" You are not ready for a question like that, way over in Africa. Basically, it's the black/white situation—they understand that something is wrong, but whatever it is that's wrong has produced American music, has produced the group that we sent. Frank Strozier, they got very uptight because they thought he was white and probably rightly so, but Frank at one point said, "I am not as black as you are," and when you see Frank he really is not as black, but he is saying, "I have a black soul," and it gets complicated, very, very, complicated, to try and describe this.

PAULINE: So we're right back to the theory, can the white man sing the blues.

OLIVER: He sure can, so it really is not a black/white thing in music. And we know that it is—the blues and jazz is black music. That we know and have established—well, there is somebody named Hugh Tracey, from South Africa, and he is trying to say that the reason whatever it is that happens in African music that makes it valid, is because it is instinctive with Africans, it's inbred.

PAULINE: The black militants in this country keep talking about their heritage, African heritage, roots, and their freedom, etc. What if these militants, or all black people, went to Africa, what do you think would happen?

OLIVER: Well, first of all, the physical trip is fantastic, once you cross the Atlantic and once you find the continent . . . I remember what happened to me. We arrived at Dakar, Senegal, about 4:10 in the morning —or maybe it was later, the sun was coming up. To see the shores of Africa, you know, it really was a moving thing. And when we got off the airplane and walked into the reception area . . . when you're in transit, you're separate from the people that are disembarking. I saw people in robes, which indicated that they were Muslim, a difference of one kind or another, from a religious point of view. Most of Africa, I would say, is essentially either animist or Muslim, or essentially Catholic.

That's Africa, also. I'm saying the guy that comes from the United States to get away from the missionary influence and the Catholics and the rest of it, will find that the people that run Africa think white, first of all. When I say "think white," I mean the African elite usually have European wives and the rest of that. They run the country and, if any control will ever be maintained at any one part, it goes through these channels.

They will also find, from a cultural point of view, that they can't relate, mainly because they wouldn't understand the differences between the Hausa tribe and the Mafi tribe and the Turek tribe and the Kumba tribe, and wherever Swahili is spoken between the tribes . . . all down there, all these tribes are so different from each other that there is no intermarriage between tribes. They are all black but somehow a Kumba would never marry a Hausa; a Hausa would never marry a Turek.

So first of all, we have this problem, now. Even if a boy finds a girl that he's in love with and he happens to be maybe from Mauritania, which is an Arab country right above Senegal, I'm afraid he can't get permission from his family and she can't get permission from her family because they are marrying out of their cultures—whatever the hang-up is.

Now, in addition to that, if he can survive the physical discomfort of living in a subtropic or even tropic, to sit on the equator when you go to Cameroon, and experience 100 percent humidity with 120 degree heat, if you can live through that, all right. Then he's going to have to learn French—that's completely alien. You meet an African and then he starts speaking French. But if you live in West Africa, if you're going to go back to your roots, you're going to find the French got there before you got there, and if you go to East Africa you'll find that the English have been there. If you go to the East and go along the other side towards the Indian Ocean, you'll find that the Portuguese have been there. Whatever Africa is, it's not what people think it is. Africa is Africa, and Africa has to be really left alone, because it's got its own problems. For instance, smallpox.

PAULINE: Are you saying, then, Oliver, that in all of Africa there is no refuge . . .

OLIVER: Just black Africa where I went. You will find refuge in Guinea, because it's a revolutionary-thinking type country. But the Russians are also there.

PAULINE: Where would, say, LeRoi Jones, want to go?

OLIVER: Wherever he wants to go.

PAULINE: And would he be accepted? Would he be happy? What would his hang-ups be in Africa? More so than in this country, do you think?

OLIVER: If he were to go to Africa he would have to understand the African.

PAULINE: Well, assuming he does understand, as he claims to understand, and that his roots are Africa. Would he be happy . . .

OLIVER: If you want to say as a genesis, for a beginning, fine. Everybody has a genesis at one point or another. The beginning has to happen somewhere. If you happen to be Irish, you know, that's where it started. But I'm saying the culture is different, vastly different, and if he hasn't made the trip, by all means he should do it. 'Cause that's the only thing that's going to open his eyes, you know. From a specific point of view, for each individual who feels he wants to get back to his roots, he should make the trip, and then decide from there.

PAULINE: Your going to Africa, has it helped you in any way in your life in the United States?

OLIVER: It's made me aware that I can't waste any more time talking about going back to my roots, because my roots are here.

PAULINE: Do you think that the introduction of black history or African history, and the study of African languages in college and high schools would be of help to the American blacks?

OLIVER: The study of languages? For instance, in one area in Africa alone there must be at least fifteen, sixteen dialects. Now if one lifetime is enough, then the study of one African language will not be enough time, okay? If you go up by the edge of the Sahara Desert, you'll find that the Mafi and Turek and the Hausa tribes all speak something completely different. If you really want to know what's happening, if you want to find out about history in Africa, the only history that is recorded is written in Arabic. So a guy that wants to find out the truth he damn well better be prepared. To go over there and say, "I'm home," is one thing, but then you have the culture to deal with, you have the physical thing to deal with, the very fact that all the tribes prefer to be left completely alone, and anybody from the States will not really be considered an outsider, but you'll never become an insider because, you know, it just isn't done.

And having a black face does not mean that it's automatic. It is simply not that way. They realize that all men are brothers somehow, but the differences from one tribe to another are immense. And Freddie Hill, the only member of the group that would get applause even when he didn't play because he was black . . . this disturbed me mainly because it occurred to me that maybe Africa is black-conscious, and then if it is, that would leave a person like me out, because like I told you before, a person of mixed blood is called a *matisse*, and not that that bothered me at all, but it occurred to me that a person like Frank Strozier, whereas . . . why should we start to define how much black blood he has in his name, because it's silly. It's a waste of everybody's time to even get involved in it.

PAULINE: Would you make the trip again, Oliver?

OLIVER: Yeah, yeah, of course I would. But I'm only going to go as a student. I'm not going to go as an active participant to, say . . . you know, I'm going to make my family learn how to speak Swahili and the rest of that. There are no Afros in Africa. The dashikis that they wear they've been wearing for a long, long time. Swahili is a word that exists only in East Africa, so if you go to North Africa, be prepared to speak some Arabic, Hausa, and Mafi; Kumba if you happen to be down in the Cameroons, and any number of African dialects in between. I mean, if you really want to get it together, one thing that the Africans use is their own music, traditional music. This is intact, it's worth that just to make the trip, just to go and hear some music that has not really succumbed to whatever it is that European or Western influences have subjected it to. That's why I say the difference between colonization and slavery obviously produced jazz, all the music that we know as American music. I don't like the word "jazz" because it doesn't cover everything.

PAULINE: If you were going to meet and talk to Stokely Carmichael, or LeRoi Jones and Archie Shepp or Rap Brown, Eldridge Cleaver, what we know as the militant movement in the United States, as one black American to another, what advice would you give to them?

OLIVER: No advice. You can't give anybody any advice. They should make the trip. They should simply make this kind of a trip.

PAULINE: I don't even mean about the trip. I mean about Americans. What is the answer for black Americans?

OLIVER: We have to develop what we have here. It's a strange thing, I mentioned this yesterday. Everybody was saying that the one thing they were able to observe was that when Malcolm X came back from Africa he was a different person. It hasn't been defined how or what it was that had made him different. But he had to make the trip, remember? And he had one musician in our group, Stanley Gilbert, who is a Muslim, you know, the American thing, Elijah Muhammad, and in Africa he found that he was accepted when he had agreed that he would learn to read and write Arabic, because what he was embracing then was not an

American kind of Islam. Islam is Islam, and it exists in Africa. So they gave him a name, and every day Stanley was out at the mosque, and he always found a friend once he let them know that he was a Muslim.

What he was trying to find out is the correlation between the American branch of Muslims and what is really happening in Africa, and he found that it was different. The one requirement, of course, is that he had to learn some Arabic, they don't think about that here, the American Muslims do not think about Arabic as being universally necessary.

PAULINE: Do you intend to salute Africa in any way in a future album?

OLIVER: Well, that's a good question. I think probably what I've learned rhythmically will be of some use to me.

PAULINE: In my lifetime I've always been taught by what I read or what I see that American jazz music is a black man's music, and it's a unique American experience; and as I delve into the subject I begin to realize that it *is* true, at least to my way of thinking, that it is a black music. It seems to me that there are no European white musicians who really can play jazz, yet there are American white musicians who play jazz only because they're American, and the American black man is responsible for jazz music.

Now up until this conversation, I've always felt in the back of my mind, based on talking to young black musicians, that black Africa is the place. That's where jazz came from and there must be a lot of great jazz musicians in Africa.

OLIVER: One of the things that we did in our concerts, every concert that we did at some point, there had to be some mention of the very fact that jazz had its beginnings in Africa. And this has to be true. From anywhere along the coast, even from the interior. Jazz had its beginning there, they were the first people who brought it to America, generally to the South. And this was our one thing that we were able to absolutely agree 100 percent on, is that its genesis was Africa. It had to be: from a physical point of view—crossing the ocean.

Now, we also went to the Virgin Islands, we went to all the islands that are French-speaking, all the islands that are English-speaking, all along that chain from Nassau to wherever the island chain goes. Now, it would have been just as easy for jazz to have started there, but somehow it didn't. African music continued in all these places. It continued in Nassau, Trinidad, Haiti, all these places, essentially high-life music, popular music, voodoo, all the music that was associated with tradition, rites, and everything else. All along this chain please remember that everything is accessible to the sea, but when it got to these shores, to American shores, something happened to it; and I'm saying the same thing again, that obviously the experience must have been slavery. That had to be the experience. But it does not deny any white person who can feel the experience. Actually it's almost a national pride. If Phil Woods plays the blues it's because he happens to be an American and he happens to play it better than most people I know.

PAULINE: Well, there are always exceptions. You mentioned Woods, when we talk about Sweden or when we talk about France, Italy, we may find today one or two musicians who . . .

OLIVER: In the whole country.

PAULINE: In the whole country, who play jazz with status that we will accept. However, in the United States we know there are more white musicians that play jazz than in all the European countries. To me, Phil Woods is still an exception. I could think of ten alto players that I think play jazz and they're all black, and then if I was going to add one or two more that are white I could squeeze in Phil Woods.

OLIVER: But now, how many black musicians, now, today, how many black musicians that advocate social change and the rest of that can play the blues? It's almost like saying the new people that have come on the scene are unable to cope with the situation, maybe because they don't understand emotionally what all that was supposed to have meant. I found jazz musicians, young guys, you ask them, "Have you ever heard of Charlie Parker?" and they will say no. It is remarkable that it is essentially American. I don't know why.

PAULINE: Well, we were just talking about the blues. We were limiting it to the blues. I'm not putting down a young black American musician just because he can't play the blues.

OLIVER: Because he doesn't understand the experience or what?

PAULINE: Well, I'm not saying he is a lesser jazz musician, but this whole thing is based on . . .

OLIVER: ⎰American music.

PAULINE: ⎱ American music. If a young black musician today doesn't understand or cannot play the blues, he's still saying something very important in that these things that he's saying may be the blues of 1969.

OLIVER: This could be true, yes.

PAULINE: Why is it that it's always the black musician that changes things or moves it in a different direction? Why is it that the only innovators are black?

OLIVER: What struggle do you have in Lapland?

PAULINE: Well, that's the point. Okay.

OLIVER: Why is it that this country is the only country that's produced it? Why is it that this country is the only country that's really multiracially oriented? Why does it happen here? No matter what's wrong with it. You don't have any social revolution in New Zealand other than the fact that nonwhites can't own property, but one day somebody's going to say why not?

PAULINE: Oliver, if your son, Chip, asked you, "Should I be a jazz musician?" what would your advice be?

OLIVER: Only if you have talent.

Horace Tapscott
Interview by Frank Kofsky

TAPSCOTT: I was born in Houston, Texas, 1934. I left there when I was about nine years old. My mother started me playing at about five or six.

KOFSKY: On piano?

TAPSCOTT: Piano. And you know, I thought that was kind of faggotty. And then I went on—you know, my mother was a musician herself, she played the piano in clubs. So, you know, naturally everything that happened, anything that was musical, she would take me to it. I went to a concert one time in Houston and the cats were playing and the trombone player was on the side and he was so masterful that I told her that's the instrument I wanted to play. That's the instrument that I got serious on up to a point.

Then I had a kidney ailment. Meanwhile, I was still on the box. I had to go back to spend more time with that. I went to the Coast, but before that I was playing my first professional job with a local cat and his name was Monroe Tucker. I was playing trombone.

KOFSKY: Did you go to high school in Los Angeles?

TAPSCOTT: I actually went to grammar school, all the way from grammar school—I got out here when I was nine years old, in 1943 or '44 during the war. I played with—you know, they had the black union then, Local 767, on Central Avenue. I lived across the street. I played over there with all the cats when they used to come around—like Gerald Wilson. Gerald Wilson is the cat that really took me off the streets and got me playing the instrument. He was the cat. He saw me when I was fifteen years old and he used to come by and pick me up and taught me how to play.

KOFSKY: You were still playing trombone then?

TAPSCOTT: I was still playing trombone. You know, I got to a point where I got to a place where I could play professional. Then I had to go to the army, to Korea. I played there, all the way through—four years—with a cat named Billy James.

Finally it got to a point where I couldn't, you know, I couldn't get any more sound from the 'bone, so I just spent most of the time playing the box. I had a little help. I started playing with different cats around the town. You know, many cats before I wouldn't be able to play with. They had to be a certain bag, to let me play with them.

KOFSKY: A certain kind of style.

TAPSCOTT: Yes, and I wasn't able to play with them too much, so I had to do my own things all the time, each time. My first good gig was at the old Troubadour. The original Troubadour on La Cienega. They didn't have anything but jazz every night. Then all the cats, Charles Lloyd—all the cats would make it down there. Jimmy Woods was the alto player.

KOFSKY: He was going to L.A. State College at the time I was teaching there about that time, right?

TAPSCOTT: Right. Well, he was in the group. We played and then I split again. This time I was traveling with vocalists and being—

KOFSKY: Backup?

TAPSCOTT: Backup vocalists for a while, mostly with Lorez Alexandria.

KOFSKY: How long were you with her?

TAPSCOTT: About a year and a half, whenever she was working. And it was a ball to play with her, because she's a musician, see? She dug the cats. Then I played with mostly local cats, things like that. But other than that, maybe every now and then I might sit with one of the cats around town, but we kept ourselves mostly on the southeast side of Los Angeles. The group we had was an underground musicians' organization. We called it UGMA—Underground Musicians Association. Most of the cats in this were young cats, or even old cats, you know, they had hangups. Their will was killed, you know? Some of the cats wouldn't let them play with them, you know, because they didn't get high together. These cats were kicking habits and doing all kind of things—they were good musicians, but you know, all they needed was some confidence in themselves. We got an organization together and we had twenty-six pieces.

KOFSKY: That was your brainchild, wasn't it?

TAPSCOTT: Yes, it was me and a chick named Linda. We talked about it and we put it in motion. It's been ever since. Naturally, there are a lot of people that are out of it now, but there's still a nucleus that's there. The whole idea now, even in these times, is to broaden the scope, tap all the resources that we have. You see we spent all of our time on 103rd Street [in the heart of Watts—F. K.] before it became fashionable. You dig?

KOFSKY: Yes.

TAPSCOTT: You know, we were rehearsing and playing along with John Carter and Bobby Bradford. We were all down there together, around the corner from each other.

KOFSKY: When did this development start? Can you put a year on it?

TAPSCOTT: Which development—where everybody's going now?

KOFSY: What I'm interested in—the thing that interested me most was UGMA.

TAPSCOTT: That's what it was.

KOFSKY: That started in '66—something like that?

TAPSCOTT: No.

KOFSKY: Before that?

TAPSCOTT: '64.

KOFSKY: As early as '64?

TAPSCOTT: Before the riots. We had a community culture center.

KOFSKY: It sounds to me, from the way you described it, as a kind of a community self-help project.

TAPSCOTT: It was. It was like to preserve music, our music, black music. In that instance, you know, none of the kids knew anything about none of the black musicians that had ever been around ever. You know, the whole idea was first to get your own thing together, any way you could to make people realize that the community supports the music as well. Because there's an area for this music. It's like this: You see how many cats are dead because they weren't supported by their own.

KOFSKY: Right.

TAPSCOTT: I mean, like it was no point in cats dying before they get to fifty. It's a bad thing, it's a *bad thing,* and it affected me and a lot of other cats—you know, a lot of other cats would give up the whole thing and go into another bag and forget about their contribution to music. That *can't happen now.*

KOFSKY: That's an aspect that I'm very curious about. It's frequently maintained, especially by a certain group of writers, that black music has no support in the black community, that it's only a bunch of white intellectuals who are interested in it. This is not what I've seen, so I wonder, since you were actually involved in a community project like this, what kind of support you did get, especially since you've been involved in it now for five years?

TAPSCOTT: Well, it was like this. When the band would come to Watts, everybody in the community knew who they were. That's the way it was. You know, the white people that came out to help support—I mean they were just music listeners. There was no *thing* happening, they actually *were* music listeners and they were *accepted* in Watts as music listeners. They knew that. There was no big thing about who came. They understood what we were trying to get our own people to realize about what they have.

Like my son, Niles, when he grows up, he *has to know.* He has to know about Duke Ellington. He has to know about Fats Waller. He has to know about Fats Navarro. He has to know about Clifford; he has to know about John. He knows about Coltrane, but I mean even back farther than that. We want him to. We're trying—we would like to do with like Bob and John and some more cats like Lester Robinson and myself and several others, Black Arthur [Arthur Blythe], you know, we would like to incorporate this as a thing in the school. But you know how? You have to do that through records. You have to do that through buying records. This is what we'd like to get us now. What makes it so good to us now, man, is the fact that it's not a competitive thing—not really. As far as we're concerned, we're making records for the cats. We know we're going to have to try to sell. All right, so sell just enough to live on—just so you can keep yourself together. You know, all your life, like myself, Sunday—Easter Sunday—I was thirty-five. I started playing when I was nine. That's my whole life and it's serious to me. It has nothing to do with who's this and who's that. I enjoy *all* the players. All the players that have something to say, I can dig. Now we have to contribute this thing and we have to hold this thing together. This is what I like to be a part of. I *have* to be a part—you know, be a part of a culture.

KOFSKY: Sure.

TAPSCOTT: You know, you have to have a thing to start from, a thing to believe in. This is not a thing of who's this and who's that. Musicians, like the Japanese musicians, when they play they're talking about something that is in their tradition, their culture. That's all they're playing about. When the Africans are playing, that's what they're playing about. Well, that's what we should be playing. That's exactly what we're here for, and we should be supported by our communities to keep our culture.

KOFSKY: Right. And you found that when you had the chance to play, you *were* being supported by the community?

TAPSCOTT: When we had the chance—we had to go through a stage of teaching, naturally. You know, we had to bring people along because, all of a sudden, all over the radio they bam, bam—like the guitars. They've been brainwashed all day with that. So they didn't have a chance to appreciate Trane—maybe Trane would have still been alive or Eric [Dolphy]—maybe these cats would have been alive if their own people first—you know, first everything has to happen economically. All these things have to happen economically. All these things have to happen together. I mean, to begin to be aware, to be aware that a giant is awakened, to be aware that things are happening, is the whole idea. If you don't have the bread and you want to do something, you're going to support us just being there, by enjoying it, by knowing—you get your point over better.

KOFSKY: Identifying with it.

TAPSCOTT: Identifying. That's what we have to do. We can't identify with just the blues. The blues stretched out from—without this, without the blues, naturally, there wouldn't have been any of what we have now. But I mean, that's just a part. We should stretch it all the way out to as far as it's supposed to go. That's the idea of my being in music, and I intend to—regardless of whatever happens or how it happens working or not working—I intend to, and I have enough support of people who believe the same way, that we're going to do this. It has to be done some way. We *love* music; we *love* our people; we *love* people. And music brings all people together. Each people who has the music that they identify themselves with more than one thing, more than one kind, more than one time—so this is for us to do.

We have so many things we have to do, and we all have to do it together. That's the way we bring about the peace and harmony that they talk about. When everybody can make it, when everybody can make it; when everybody has just enough to make it. And back to music, when everybody realizes what's happening. Like when your grandson hears Coltrane, or some records, he *knows*—he knows the history about the culture. It's there. He can go and refer to it in the library.

KOFSKY: Right.

TAPSCOTT: Or in school.

KOFSKY: Right.

TAPSCOTT: And music appreciation. When I was going to school, I dug Beethoven and all the cats. But see, I should have been listening to Duke Ellington in school too, as well. I should have been listening to all the other cats. There are some cats I don't even know about, man, who've been playing. Some guys have got records out that I've never heard of. But not again. This shouldn't happen again. I don't imagine it will, with all the ways things are today. We're going to do it, but if we do it, we have to do it through the right channels. And that's through the Board of Education. That's one of the best ways, and that's where our music has to get into. Presently, you have to rely on best-sellers, to make it.

KOFSKY: Are you a teacher like John [Carter] and Bobby [Bradford]?

TAPSCOTT: No, though I teach a class of theory at Grant's Music Center. I teach there every Saturday. I teach the cats just about as far as applying, practical appreciation of their music, their knowledge of music. Some of them have been going to conservatories, which I don't knock, but I mean these cats, they don't know anything about the conservatory because their school is the streets. So I mean, here we are, we can do these things here, we can get the thing together. I teach this on Saturdays at the Black Student Union. They asked me if Bobby Bradford couldn't make a thing, would I make it. I said, yeah, but it was good that Bobby made it because it's all in the same thing. I would look forward to doing that as far as young musicians. I also look forward to having this orchestra that's here for the community —that the community supports.

KOFSKY: So you definitely approve of what the BSU, the various Black Students Unions, are doing in terms of making people more aware of their heritage.

TAPSCOTT: Definitely.

KOFSKY: In fact, you were thinking along those lines before they were even—

TAPSCOTT: Yes. And the younger ones carried the thought on with more action. My kids—I've got a fourteen-year-old son and a sixteen-year-old daughter. And I mean they're right there; they're right in it. This is the way they're thinking. Perhaps if they had thought that way when I was coming up, I would have, we all would have been in better shape. We wouldn't have to be going through them unnecessary things like wars and things, you know. But see, it's all part of it and the music is part of everything—just like everything, it's part of everything.

KOFSKY: That's just what Coltrane said, too, when I asked him about that.

TAPSCOTT: Yes. This is what it really is—it's a part of all. When I first heard the *Spiritual,* Coltrane's *Spiritual,* I was in New York on a date. I was with Lionel Hampton. That Sunday afternoon we went there and they recorded that and immediately after, all over the country, it started happening. I mean it happened a little before, naturally, but I mean *after* that, that sound got across I imagine. It got all over the country and everybody thought "Ah, music—the music." And the music had a lot to do with everything. You know how they don't like you to play certain music in certain places, because, you know. So I really—I know, that's one of the first things that we have to get together. We have to have more *respect* for music. We can't take music for granted. From what we hear—the radio, the commercials, the commercial outlets that we have, and the mass media—that's what kills. We need more people in there who are for real. I mean for real, you know, for everybody. I think that will be hip, and I'm glad there are the kind that even the television shows are doing—I'm glad, I'm glad because it helps. That means it brings in more of the real thing. And if everybody's living off the real thing, we can do anything we want to.

KOFSKY: How did you get thinking along those lines? I've been doing interviews for a long time on black nationalism and the music. Some guys will just say, "Well man, I don't concern myself with politics and so forth; I just want to play my music," and so on, and so on. You don't seem to be thinking along those lines. You seem to be thinking in a much more political sense. That is, you really see the music as part of a general culture and realize that the culture has to preserve the music or the music will die. I'm wondering as to how you became aware of this, because I'm trying to understand the people who *aren't* aware of it and why they're not. Maybe if I understand why you are, I'll understand why they're not.

TAPSCOTT: I don't know. I guess it's because I began to realize you learn things as you go, if you try. If you keep your eyes and ears open. I've been trying to see why different things—why did my father leave home? The music is beautiful, but without the life, there would be no music.

KOFSKY: That's right. But a lot of people don't seem to understand that. They seem to want to divorce the music from the social structure.

TAPSCOTT: I don't think they can—whomever that may be, however they might think that is, perhaps. If that's really the way they think, then that's it. Then that's really what's happening. But to me, I believe that all of this is a part—if the political part of it gets together and the music part of it gets together, the economic part of it gets together. The people who believe in this country that this music is in, are the ones who can let the music out, or keep it shut up. If we have these things, that people appreciate art and culture in these offices, instead of the way that they are now . . .

KOFSKY: Right.

TAPSCOTT: Then, I mean, it would be very simple. The cats would be like it is overseas--I don't know how they're subsidized in different countries. All right, we know that's solid. That's okay, because all the cats have to do is play. They say that we want to try this over here, well then it will be free enterprise.

KOFSKY: That's right. They would call it socialism, or something like that, if musicians were subsidized.

TAPSCOTT: All right, that's all right.

KOFSKY: But they don't say that when they give it to a missile company.

TAPSCOTT: Right. That's why it got to me. I *know* that there's a lot of bread here. I *know* my ancestors have made some of the bread here.

KOFSKY: That's right.

TAPSCOTT: And I want part of it, you know? I want part of it, to help make this what it is, what it's supposed to be. As long as this is not what it's supposed to be, I can never be completely satisfied. Nor anyone like me—white or black—they can never be completely satisfied.

KOFSKY: They can never be completely satisfied with the way things are now.

TAPSCOTT: But the whole issue is, if the cat has to put the emphasis on this thing—some of them call it hate; I'm sorry that they call it hate, I'm sorry that they don't understand. But the whole emphasis is—like if you're going to get your house together, you know what happens in your house, you know how to clean your house, you know what is in your house; you know how to do it. So you have to take certain things to do so.

This is what's happening with us. I'm very happy—I'm very happy that the group and I had a chance to record—Black Arthur and the cats. We were very happy for this. But if we hadn't have recorded, we still would have been doing the same thing. And we still will, even if we don't record again. We'll keep this going, because this is what's really happening and this is what we believe in. Once you believe in it, you feel better—anything you play is real. You don't have to make compromises. You can play. You don't have to worry about who's going to dig it. Because if a part of them identify with it—I mean, they don't have to dig it personally, but they know what it is, you know, they know what it means, at least.

Some think we're a bunch of junkies and like that, and that we don't have no responsibility. Think of us as people. Think of us as interpreters of a people. We think of ourselves as storytellers.

KOFSKY: A voice of the people.

TAPSCOTT: Voice of the people, as well. In all ways, the arts is the voice of the people, so why not utilize it while it's here, live, alive, not dead? Don't make any kind of thing of after he's gone. He's here *now*. Duke Ellington is here *now,* man. Let's praise him now. Let's praise what he has to offer and given to the world. There's nothing— he don't have to speak about Black Power or nothing. He don't have to do that. Before I was born, he was writing *Black, Brown and Beige* about his own people. I mean, people are all peoples, and learn to appreciate that because they understand.

KOFSKY: Almost all people.

TAPSCOTT: Well, you know.

KOFSKY: But when it came to the Pulitzer Prize in music in 1966, they turned him down. They didn't award a prize that year. So, *some* people appreciate him. Unfortunately, not as many as should.

TAPSCOTT: And he's been out there for thirty years.

KOFSKY: Yes, if not more.

TAPSCOTT: He's still creative, so I mean, why shouldn't the rest of them merit that voice? I know naturally that a certain area had to be hit . . . a cat brings some poison in the neighborhood and you get hit. But that's a thing of the past almost.

KOFSKY: It *should* be a thing of the past. Besides, that's just the way of avoiding the ugliness of the situation. Whereas perhaps it's better, healthier, to confront that situation directly and look at it for what it is, than it is to poison yourself so you don't have to see it.

TAPPSCOTT: Yes, since you're going to be in it. I mean if you're not going to be in it, just jump off the river. Because you want the benefits from it, so I mean you got to pay the dues for it. That's the way we have to see it. We have to see that what we want, we have to pay the dues for. I think, all in all, it's a beautiful life, because I really enjoy working out there every day and being around people that I know dig me and love me. These are *my* people. These are real people. These are my family. I don't have to be starving. Because you know, I *have* starved according to certain levels, but as far as I'm concerned, I've always had something I can do to keep myself—you know, to go on. If I can do that, I can do it wrong and I can even do it better if I keep doing it long enough. And I intend to. That's the whole idea, in a nutshell.

Gary Bartz
by David C. Hunt

In a 1961 letter to a major jazz publication, composer-arranger Ernie Wilkins lamented the upsurge of contemporary jazz "hippies," when he wrote; "Oh, they can wail! Can play 'double-ups' all night long. Tempos can't get too fast, they know all the fashionable licks, know all of the solos on records, and keep up with the latest trends. But what, at base, are they saying of their own?"

In no way can alto saxophonist Gary Bartz be considered a contemporary jazz hippie. He gives each performance a kind of superior coherence of its own, one that is hardly implicit in the original melody of a composition and in no way dependent on the harmonic framework. By getting inside a theme, he can distill its essence and use it as a basis for improvisation—without merely embellishing it in the decorative sense of abandoning it totally. Thus Bartz does say something of his own.

Not only does Bartz possess the emotional impact, power, and sureness of a major jazz artist, he is, in addition, deliberate and elegantly introspective, showing a commendable restraint at crucial moments when rapid technical execution can become expression itself in the hands of a lesser talent. His statements of directness and simplicity are made with just enough pitch variation and rhythmic subtlety to give them a high degree of internal tension.

At one point in his career, the young altoist readily admitted being under the influence of Sonny Rollins. Although he doesn't directly imitate Rollins' sound now, he does make a personal translation of the tenor saxophonist's rhythmic energy and sense of structure. The most interesting aspect of Bartz's individual growth out of the Rollins bag, however, lies not in his variance of the timing and inflection of notes, but rather in the velocity with which he chooses to improvise. It could be said that he plays alto with a distinct tenor feeling. He shows very little predilection for "Bird flights" and utilizes many sustained tones in his choruses.

All of these artistic assets point toward a highly satisfying personal style—one which is very much in evidence with the release of Bartz's recent album *Another Earth* (Milestone MSP 9018). As with every Bartz effort, each interdependent movement of this extended composition is well conceived, musically and artistically. The piece, as a whole, is very realistic from the standpoint of music produced for a particular symbolic purpose. All of the razor-sharp solos and bridging passages by

Bartz, alto sax; Charles Tolliver, trumpet; Pharaoh Sanders, tenor sax; Stanley Cowell, piano; Reggie Workman, bass; and Freddy Waits, drums, are beautifully executed translations of space phenomena, from the smallest star to the largest galaxy. The feeling of other-worldiness is not overdone for the sake of effect alone; it is incorporated into the improvisatory projection of each player. This in itself is a tribute to Bartz as a composer.

Bartz's wife, Maxine, pinpointed his motivation for the album theme when she wrote in the detailed liner notes:

"Life—the Great Miracle, as symbolized by the vastness and wonder of interstellar space and worlds undiscovered, is the theme of this album. This personal tribute by Gary is the direct result of a period of dual exploration of music and the heavens sparked by two important acquisitions: a telescope (after years of paperback study of astronomy) and a piano (after years of composing within the limits of the alto saxophone)."

Side two of the album is composed of four original tunes by Bartz, all maintaining the same space sound and showcasing him as the only horn soloist. He proves here that he has the ability to sustain a consistently high level of artistic creation and musical interest. He is, in fact, one of the very few horn soloists to emerge in the sixties who has a definite potential to play solo horn without any other instrumental backing.

Bartz's introductory album on Milestone, *Libra* (MSP 9006), spotlighted him as the leader of an explosive quintet featuring Jimmy Owens, trumpet and Flügelhorn; Albert Daily, piano; Richard Davis, bass; and Billy Higgins, drums. The highlight of this session, aside from Bartz's most memorable moments on record thus far, is the unusual degree of melodic content in both compositions and solos. The listener will find himself humming snatches of "Eastern Blues," "Disjunction," "Air and Fire," "Libra," and "Freedom One Day" after just the first hearing. The whole album makes one want to hear it again and again.

Orrin Keepnews, Milestone records producer, said of the session: "This is, at its core, melodic jazz! and it is basically happy music. Not in any simple-minded, gee whiz sort of way, for there is much complexity and thought here. But there is also a distinct feeling of pleasure; these are men who like to play and don't mind a bit if you enjoy listening."

In contrast to the version contained in Bartz's own album, "Libra" becomes a syncopated strut under the leadership of drummer Max Roach in the Atlantic recording, *Members, Don't Git Weary* (SD 1510). Bartz is launched into a soaring solo by the masterful drummer, but seems less comfortable than in front of Richard Davis' dancing bass lines on the Milestone cut. Noticeable in all of his solos on this album is a tendency toward note economy while favoring an unhurried approach to harmonic interpretation.

Bartz also makes excellent contributions to the Art Blakey Jazz Messengers album *Soul Finger* (Limelight LS 86018), featuring Lucky

Thompson, Freddie Hubbard, and Lee Morgan, and to Roy Ayers's tasteful album, *Stone Soul Picnic* (Atlantic SD 1514). Listeners interested in Bartz; Charles Tolliver, trumpet; Hubert Laws, flute; Herbie Hancock; Ron Carter and Miroslav Vitous, bass; and Grady Tate, drums, shouldn't be put off by the cover of the latter album. The music is extremely satisfying.

That Bartz was continually probing, exploring, and developing the essences of good solo structure and jazz composition became evident when he was a youthful musician in Baltimore, where he was born on September 26, 1940. He cites recordings by Count Basie, Louis Jordan, Dizzy Gillespie, and Charlie Parker as being responsible for his early awareness of jazz and remembers thinking that Parker's sound was "the prettiest thing I'd ever heard." Bartz came to New York when he was seventeen years old and studied extensively at Juilliard. He has worked with Art Blakey's Jazz Messengers, Max Roach, and many first-rate players who came to Baltimore.

It is apparent from his background and past artistic achievements that Gary Bartz is an important creative jazzman intent on communicating his symbolic messages through strict musical values, without commercial gimmickry. As a result, he travels the more difficult road to success. But Bartz will continually reach out from within—producing arresting and provocative art music in search of the recognition he so richly deserves.

Coleman, Coltrane, and Shepp: The Need for An Educated Audience
by David C. Hunt

Throughout jazz history, the outstanding innovators have been those artists who reshaped past conventions by discovering startling new ways of structuring musical forms, making technical advances, or proclaiming social symbolism in their individual modes of expression. As a result, these innovators place staggering demands on the listener. Familiar or imaginable sounds based on previous aesthetic standards have become unrecognizable in the total experimentation they sustain while immersing themselves in a new vision or reflection of society. Awakening the obvious or the basic in their audience at a crucial point in innovation results in severe restrictions in the inner search and hence remains unthinkable.

But what of the potential jazz audience? A hard look at the gap between Ornette Coleman, John Coltrane, Archie Shepp, and the majority of listeners shows conclusively that their innovations are conceived as the special property of an artistically minded minority and, also, that the most essential rudiments of their genius are still misunderstood or ignored. A larger, more appreciative audience for these contemporary innovators cannot be cultivated merely through their recordings and personal appearances; an extensive jazz education program complete with musically illustrated lectures and workshops is sorely needed to expose their artistry and preserve the continued growth of jazz as an art form.

For example, tenor saxophonist Archie Shepp is one of the most controversial jazz artists ever to appear on the American scene. His seemingly authoritarian views on what jazz should be to other musicians, how it should be played, and how the white man should feel about it constitute a hard-line artistic and social philosophy provoking immediate response from anyone seriously concerned about the future of jazz. The extremism which Shepp exhibits triggers equally extreme reactions. There is no middle ground. You either worship him or you hate him.

Shepp's feelings about the music he plays run something like this:

"Music must at times terrify! If must shake men by the throats. It must extol the inevitable triumph of full stomachs and fat laughing babies. It must bring social as well as aesthetic order to our lives. Sometimes we must bludgeon beauty to seeming death; make it ugly; simply because life itself is at times ugly and painful to behold."

This is Archie Shepp's conception as a responsible spokesman to his fellow men. His feelings are admirable; unfortunately he hasn't cleared the air through his social commentary or his musicianship. The manner in which he chooses to project these thoughts through his horn continues to irritate and confuse the average listener. Shepp must make an effort to explain how his razor-sharp social philosophy relates to his musical conception. Thousands of jazz fans will hear him play who have never read one of his magazine articles.

The whole New Thing movement presupposes that anyone who listens to the music can instantly interpret the vastly complex psyches of the artists creating it. In an article in the defunct *Sounds and Fury* magazine, "Joy in the New Music," Joe Pinelli states: "It's true that it helps in retrospect to be able to say what a musician has done in technical terms, but that's primarily for other musicians, not for the listener whose only concern is how the music makes him feel . . . ." In a review of *Spiritual Unity,* a provocative album by the Albert Ayler trio, Mort Maizlish summarizes the New Thing by confidently stating, "Anyone can understand it; all human beings who know their own emotions will know what it means."

If a large segment of the jazz audience is to hear the New Thing in terms they understand, the music as a definitive reflection of the modern Negro psychology—the suffering, protest, and self-determination that the people feel—must be communicated verbally and in much less abstract terminology than has been employed to date by its advocates. Often forgotten by critics and musicians alike is the sad reality that our educational system does not provide the majority of human beings it serves with an awareness of nonverbal forms of expression.

Likewise, it is not easy to glance backward at the tempest of controversy Ornette Coleman provoked in the late fifties when one realizes how little has actually been exposed about the music he plays. The naked emotional power he unleashes, through a form devoid of most traditional guideposts, is still a major factor in his controversial status today. Coleman freely described this phenomenon of "human pitch" in interviews and magazine articles; but without actual demonstrations in musical terms, much of his verbal descriptions fell on deaf ears.

Ornette Coleman's seemingly free improvisations stem from the fact that he has fused both the vertical and horizontal approaches of playing into a kind of tonal gravity relative to existing vertical and horizontal tonal centers. This all-encompassing relativity almost eliminates the right or wrong of Coleman's melodic invention in favor of a close-to-distant approach to tonal centers.

George Russell seems to have most approximated Coleman's personal jazz philosophy in an article by Martin Williams, "Ornette Coleman and Tonality," in the old *Jazz Review* magazine:

"Ornette seems to depend mostly on the overall tonality of the song as a point of departure for melody. By this I don't mean the key the music might be in. His pieces don't readily infer key. They could almost be in any key or no key. I mean that the melody and the chords of his compositions have an overall sound which Ornette seems to use as a point of departure. This approach liberates the improviser to sing his own song really, without having to meet the deadline of any particular chord."

Failure to expose the relationship between Coleman's personal philosophy and the resulting translation of it into musical values through any real educational means gave rise to serious misconceptions and widespread speculations. John Tynan reported Coleman's artistic mission as "personal" and said that it "served his own bright muse." Coleman immediately became a most promising recording property as others cried "fraud," "genius," "unbearable nonsense," "another Bird."

In an article "Cannonball Looks at Ornete Coleman," Julian Adderley stated: "The improvisation seemed inconsistent with both the implied chords of the melodic line and those played in accompaniment by the pianist." This observation was just one in the landslide of criticism clearly suggesting that Coleman's solos did not have a relationship to themes previously stated. Although each situation warrants individual consideration, one can certainly relate to the basic pitch, emotion, rhythm, or even melody of a theme without relating to its actual chord changes.

The fact that established artists Cannonball Adderley, Dizzy Gillespie, Roy Eldridge, and Paul Chambers either could not, or would not, give clear explanations of Ornette Coleman's improvisational flights, even in musical terms, cast a questionable shadow over the new music. It continued to be described in negative terms—squeaking, neighing, honking. Most observers felt that Coleman championed an art form that few could feel, understand, or discuss. Even getting a feeling of the total performance, other than anger or rejection, became a problem for almost every listener.

The gradual ascendance of tenor saxophonist John Coltrane to the forefront of contemporary jazz as a fresh voice in the most rapidly growing of all creative languages posed many musical problems for his audience. Though Coltrane took almost four years to develop his harmonically dense approach to playing (popularly termed "sheets of sound"), most listeners fell by the wayside in the first two years. As an artist endowed with a potentially fantastic harmonic ear, Coltrane chose a completely personal approach to his playing, even in his earliest 1954 days with the Miles Davis quintet.

More controversial than his harmonic explorations to most listeners were three standard qualities—technique, tone, and intonation. Coltrane had, at the time, a full three-octave range upward from concert A flat, with equal strength in all registers. But his technical approach was severely criticized by many who resented his seemingly nervous "running the horn." Problematic in his early stages with Miles Davis was his insistence on doing harmonic homework on the stand nightly. Though receiving a substantial amount of bitter complaints, Davis was patient—and Coltrane grew with justifiable self-confidence.

Coltrane's tone, called by mainstreamers pinched and too searing, resulted from the particular reed and mouthpiece chosen, plus an extremely tight embouchure. To jazz fans and musicians who claim that the tone of Sonny Rollins, Stan Getz, or Coleman Hawkins is a good saxophone sound, one can only add that a sound must suit a player's conception. A good sound is open to interpretation from many angles. His intonation has always been questioned due to a sharp edge in his sound, but he consistently played in tune until his death.

Harmonically, he began with a thirst for experimenting with unusual chord extensions and alterations. Listeners frequently shook their heads claiming Coltrane to be "blowing outside the chord changes" or "just running a bunch of scales," and these criticisms have often been justified. But he pushed ahead, feverishly proving that his irregularly accented arhythmic phrases could be things of beauty in more polished form.

The three periods in Coltrane's harmonic quest began in 1955 with the Miles Davis quintet. The first period with Davis was one of basic groping for his own voice. Many performances, though otherwise artistically satisfying, were spoiled by his uncertainty.

By mid-1957, when he joined the Thelonious Monk quartet, Coltrane was on solid ground with multinoted thinking. Monk reportedly stimulated his interest in the sounding of more than one note simultaneously through false fingering and lip adjustments. More important, Coltrane had the opportunity to apply his reversible five-note chords and long lines of rapid-fire sixteenth and thirty-second notes to Monk's ingenious compositions.

Upon leaving Monk, Coltrane returned to the Miles Davis group. He now leaned heavily in the direction of playing the entire scale of each chord. Phrasing in uneven groups of fives and sevens became common. Though furiously engaged in utilizing sound, rhythm, and harmony in this deeply personal artistry, Davis' modal linear designs made a permanent imprint on his later architectural extensions as leader of his own quartet.

Coltrane's quartet recording of "My Favorite Things," from Rodgers and Hammerstein's hit show, *The Sound of Music,* brought him a public acceptance that, in less than two years, clouded over into a storm of bewilderment and doubt from many quarters. Coltrane's presentations were said to have been abstracted from less familiar reference, even though the standard format of introducing a clearly defined song form from which to solo has always been maintained. Most critics of these abstract performances complained bitterly of being unable to hear logical improvisations from what he played, and felt they were being cheated out of a finished work by what was considered practicing in public. To further complicate matters, Coltrane recorded a version of "Greensleeves" which contained a different set of chord changes for the order of solos than were implied by the statement of the melody.

Coltrane himself admitted the need for solo editing, but spoke of the length of his solos as a need to attempt to recapture the fleeting spontaneity that deserts any jazz improviser in the course of an evening. Even though an experimenting artist must consider that his ideas have not necessarily matured to the point where they are ready for public scrutiny, it is difficult to expect him to forsake his own personal daring for polished performances.

In tribute, Coltrane was the supreme creative artist whose conscience bound him to the highest plateau of human fulfillment in his work. He could not do less for the sake of commercialism or mass appeal. He could not sin against his art. That which is grotesque, outrageous, and repulsively ugly must be symbolized musically and projected realistically in the jazz form. Coltrane shattered the commonly held naive conception that beauty should be projected through an art medium in positive values only. He consistently communicated love in his improvisations to a point of realistic perfection unsurpassed in contemporary jazz.

The human community needs the beauty and the truth of the contemporary jazz artist's own singular message, but today's community has not, for the most part, consented to the intentions of Coleman and Shepp any more than the community of the forties championed Parker and Gillespie or the general public of the fifties knew and accepted Coltrane. The question of how to instill this need for and recognition of beauty and truth in a larger segment of the human community has plagued artists, critics, writers, and record producers since jazz ceased to be dancing music in the early forties. Leonard Bernstein tackled the problem in more general terms when he discussed the music education of the layman in the introduction to his provocative book, *The Joy of Music*. He outlined the problem in the following manner:

"Obviously we can't use musical terminology exclusively, or we will simply drive the victim away. We must have intermittent recourse to certain extramusical ideas, like religion, or social factors, or historical forces, which may have influenced music. We don't ever want to talk down; but how *up* can we talk without losing contact? There is a happy medium somewhere between the music appreciation racket and purely technical discussion; it is hard to find, but it can be found. . . ."

Before Bernstein's "happy medium" presentation can be utilized to greatest advantage, an educational program must be organized by modern jazz artists and the supporting jazz business structure, plus outside sponsorship, aimed at securing a larger segment of the human community as a future audience.

From the educational standpoint, most artists have continually looked down on their audience as possessing little in the way of musical or artistic perception. But if jazz continues its present philosophy of indifference to the type and size of the audience it maintains, it will be in great danger of losing its already declining position as a valid art form in our society. Even now the largest percentage of jazz aficionados are members of a fringe audience whose values are easily influenced by new and dramatic developments, regardless of musical content. The artist obviously knows his own language best and must share in the responsibility of making it known to a wider audience.

Coleman, Coltrane, and Shepp have been the profound jazz commentators of the 1960s—reflecting the strength, weakness, joy, and sorrow of the society in which they live. Everyone who is touched by contemporary jazz in any way must respond to the challenge of having the maximum number in the human community understand them as such.

Byard Lancaster
Interview by John Szwed

(Byard Lancaster is typical of the new jazzman—typical of the new *musician*—in that he sees his role in life to be larger than that of entertainer, or even that of artist. Where an earlier generation of musicians saw themselves as somewhat tragic scufflers and defenders of the music of the "outsider," Lancaster wants desperately to reach all audiences with his music. To do this, he has been willing to play all kinds of music without a feeling of compromise. In fact, many younger musicians show the same commitment to their listeners that a long-gone age had when they played rent parties, street corners, or for their neighbors' entertainment. Music, for Lancaster, is a necessity of life . . . and if all men do not share it, then life is so much the worse for all.

Byard Lancaster can be heard on his own LP, Vortex 2003, *It's Not Up to Us.*)—J. S.

SZWED: The first thing I'd like to ask you, what's the earliest thing you can remember liking in music?

LANCASTER: Just music. My whole family plays. Started playing the piano when I was seven and switched to the saxophone six months later. My sister is a music teacher, Mary Ann Tyler Lancaster. And my five nieces are taking piano lessons from her. I think everybody should play because this is a form of expression.

SZWED: How about the first jazz?

LANCASTER: Fourteen. Started playing locally here in Philadelphia with J. R. Mitchell. He's a very fine drummer.

SZWED: You were just kids then?

LANCASTER: Well, I was fourteen. He's a couple of years older.

SZWED: Let me mention some people in and out of jazz, and you tell me if you remember them having any influence at all, regardless of whether you like them or not.

LANCASTER: Okay.

SZWED: Let's see. How about early James Moody before he had anything to do with Dizzy Gillespie?

LANCASTER: Not at the time. Because I didn't hear him at that time—later. On the first record given to me by my brother—Sonny Stitt—is when I started. And I went from Stitt to Paul Desmond and then to Jackie McLean. I like all three of them now. Later, Hank Crawford and Ornette Coleman and Eric Dolphy. You know, I'm developing—trying to develop a universal sound.

SZWED: You only missed Johnny Hodges out of all of that.

LANCASTER: Yeah, well I'm going into Bird and him now, I didn't study Bird either.

SZWED: Yeah, but you had Sonny Stitt who's the right-hand man. Have you been fond of Sonny Criss since he's had a comeback?

LANCASTER: I haven't heard him.

SZWED: I just saw him—unfortunately—against Roland Kirk. I have yet to see anybody who can stand up under Roland Kirk whether they are playing better than he or not. He always wins. So on volume alone, Kirk outblew him and so he got out.

LANCASTER: Well, he could. But I remember one time I played with him where he didn't because I was so young. But Roland gave me quite a few opportunities to sit in with him and to teach me quite a few lessons and so I know what you mean, because nobody can outplay what he's really doing, which is really playing.

SZWED: Well, one of the complaints that was made a few years ago was that it was tough to play with anybody, you know, unless you were in with them financially, and that young guys in New York would go up to see Miles Davis—I don't want to mention him particularly—but go up to see people and say, "So and so sent me over," and he'd say "Who are you, man?" You know, brush him off. Whereas twenty or thirty years ago, it was standard procedure to have a ring of tables around the bandstand and musicians would sit in. If you couldn't make it you didn't play any more, but you had a chance.

LANCASTER: Well, with Miles it's about fifteen years ago he started that maybe, and this is fifteen years later and things change. Everybody I've asked, but him, let me sit in—Sonny Stitt, Roland Kirk, and quite a few others—knew Cecil Taylor and he used to come by the school to give me lessons when I was in Berklee and we would hang out for a couple of minutes and quite a few other jazz musicians—Hank Crawford, you know, taught me a couple of things. So that's just one of Miles's pet peeves and he has to do what he feels. In fact after Coltrane died, quite a few musicians overplayed themselves in not knowing how to sit in with the new music and that's very difficult—just sitting in, let alone what they were playing. But they played too long or, you know, went the whole thing.

SZWED: I'd better get some more facts before we get hung up. You said you went away to school at eighteen. Where?

LANCASTER: I went to Shaw University in Raleigh, North Carolina, for one year and to Berklee for four years, and two of them—that is two more, I was in Boston Conservatory.

SZWED: What was your major at Berklee?

LANCASTER: Music education.

SZWED: Music education? You were going to teach?

LANCASTER: Yes, I was, but it really came out that I was going to play.

SZWED: There were a lot of fine musicians who did the same thing.

LANCASTER: Well, now, I have over two-hundred students. I feel that I can give them a music lesson in three or four hours to last six or seven months. And it's like, maybe, Aristotle, and the old times, when they would hang out, just teach and hang out for a whole day or I might have two or three students on the same day. It wouldn't matter. I am teaching them and am learning from them and they're learning from me.

SZWED: Do you think that the university courses were of any use to you in what you're doing now?

LANCASTER: Everything I came in contact with was helping me, but like, Berklee was really out of sight to learn music values. The conservatory taught about Bach and Beethoven, but like, the students I have now I teach about today and then go back; instead of going back and then come to date.

SZWED: Roland Kirk had the same kind of experience, you know. I knew him in Columbus, and he went to Central State College and he had special training, but he was going through the same thing you are, the idea that it's good stuff to go back to after the young people come in.

LANCASTER: Check it out.

SZWED: I don't know how many years you have to go back for this, but in recent years, anyway, in black music it's the thing that LeRoi Jones has talked about. Unifying the whole scene in one bag, and he says that if you hear what James Brown does on a horn it scares you. You know, it's all one kind of scene. Do you feel this kind of influence cutting back and forth?

LANCASTER: Well, we don't have to go back too far because I saw LeRoi a short time ago and I listen to James Brown just before I go to most of my jobs. I have one of the records that he did at the Apollo—*Night Train*—but the black musicians need to unite immediately and then black and white musicians unite and at the same time we should cut it down to the black jazz musicians and the white jazz musicians and then add on the ones in the psychedelic field; in other words, with the jazz musicians that's even with cats up to a certain age or a mood, because we need to get the new music over and that's what we're doing. So, therefore, there are very few of us.

SZWED: Do you like the idea of the guilds that have been tried in Chicago and in New York?

LANCASTER: As long as they permit musicians to work. I haven't looked into them too much, but they have to be very flexible. Because I like to work with everyone.

SZWED: You knew, anyway, that there were hassles about them, for just the reasons you're mentioning. Cats went to work and they said it's beneath them and the guy said it wasn't beneath him, that's the thing he wanted to do and—

LANCASTER: Well, that hangs it up, because who can judge? But it can only be creative, so like—no, I don't go for that.

SZWED: Continue naming some names. Cecil Taylor? Taking non-saxophonists.

LANCASTER: Cecil was the biggest influence until I heard Dave Burrell, and I heard Dave get it together on piano. I would like to play with Cecil and in fact I plan to go to New York to ask him if I can do some music with him. I respect him very much and have been listening to him for five or six years, ever since I was in Berklee. So he's out of sight and I met him a couple of times and it was very beautiful.

SZWED: You think it would be difficult to play with him? That he's the strongest piano player in the country?

LANCASTER: I don't think he's the strongest piano player in the country, but—

SZWED: Let me revise that. His accompanying is one of the most— what's the word I want? You know, he's with you as much as anybody going.

LANCASTER: Well, no, not if you've heard Dave Burrell, but Cecil is really the strongest *recorded* piano player. Dave Burrell is the same age I am, we went to Berklee together, you know, like, he learned from Cecil which is a new product of Cecil, you know, with himself.

SZWED: I was going to move across instruments. Let's just think of some drummers. Milford Graves.

LANCASTER: Sunny Murray.

SZWED: Yes. Milford and Sunny come on. The two schools of drums.

LANCASTER: Well, I don't know if they're the two schools, because I haven't heard anybody do anything that Sunny has done. I was playing with him and I heard Milford a couple of times and there's also De Johnette.

SZWED: Beaver Harris.

LANCASTER: Beaver. I worked with him, with Archie right after Martin Luther King died. And Rashied [Ali], of course. But Sunny Murray's got it.

SZWED: It's too bad he's not on more records.

LANCASTER: Sunny? Sunny has twenty-one out.

SZWED: Yes. But you know, I mean, his own records.

When you're playing along—with one other wind instrument, does it change your playing, and I'm not talking about the player now, but the instrument. If it's a trombone or a trumpet. Do you feel a different sense of where you're going just because it happens to be a reed or brass?

LANCASTER: Yes, I guess you could say that. When I'm playing with Larry Young on organ, I use the biggest mouthpiece I can get, which is a metal thing that I have, and a strong reed—the strongest possible control on the metal mouthpiece. I use different types of mouthpieces and a different type of reed for different occasions. There is always a difference, because I tend to overshadow one trombone and another saxophone.

SZWED: Well, you know, one of the things in the history of jazz —from the beginning, the trumpet was the lead instrument and it faded quickly into the saxophone after Coleman Hawkins. Saxophones have set the pace for jazz since Coleman Hawkins. You know, always in the front. Do you have any comments on that? I've never talked to saxophonists about it.

LANCASTER: We will continue to set the pace. [Laughter.] We just got it now, but also we're not just going to play one saxophone. I might play all of them; in fact, I've played baritone and alto. Also, like flute has something to say and so do the other reed instruments.

SZWED: I have often wondered why. I have picked up the saxophone and played it and found that it was an easy instrument to get a sound from and a hard one to control the sounds with. Do you know what I mean? I don't know if you ever remember picking up a reed instrument, but I imagine you're like me and you got a sound out of it right away, the mouth, but when I tried to get some control on the vibrato and so on it wasn't there. But with the trombone, you could take the slide and you could shake it with the trumpet and you take the whole horn and it seemed to me that the big difference was there, that if you were a young player you could pick up the saxophone and feel that you might make it somehow with it, and even before you could. On the brass instrument, nothing comes out but a big glob of air and you say the hell with it.

LANCASTER: Well, yeah, I really believe that. The saxophone is really closer to what's happening today and it was invented around 1830. Every person I have given lessons to—a lot of them are children —can usually get a sound out of it. I have seen quite a few girls get sounds out of it immediately. Yes, enthusiasm is more important than the techniques.

SZWED: Well, there are very few girls playing saxophone or any instrument for that reason. I saw Vi Reed some time ago and I had forgotten how strong she was.

LANCASTER: I haven't heard her yet. I have to check her out.

SZWED: She starts out strong—she was with Diz, the thing of sitting in with him, but I realize just how few chicks have played, and I think they could play.

LANCASTER: Oh, they could do anything they wanted to. In fact, that all goes back to the human mind not being developed enough or half as much as we can develop the human mind. So there's no thing about a girl playing piano or drums or sax. You know, she just has to want to do it and not listen to what has been put down before. For instance, a trumpet player will say you can't play flute because it's going to blow your harmony. I have a pretty good sound on both instruments myself. So, like, those rules are forgotten and this is a psychedelic age.

SZWED: Benny Carter played trumpet, flute, saxophone, trombone, and everything else and did pretty good on all. In fact, it's said by his friends that he went for three years without picking one up and picked it up—

LANCASTER: Yes, well, it's your approach. If you don't tell the child that bass clarinet is hard to play he'll pick it up—say, nine or ten years old. I have a student who does that and he didn't know that there should be squeaks and things like that and there weren't any.

SZWED: I had a teacher of the trombone here in town and he was telling me about how to hold your cheeks and he said the one thing you never do is let your cheeks blow out; then he looked out the window and said, "unless you're Dizzy Gillespie." I sort of dropped it there and, of course, I didn't get the point until a few years later. The point is if you can do it, you do it and if you can't do it, you don't do it. And Gillespie blows his cheeks and neck and everything out and it's like a balloon. He does it and it's unorthodox. Somebody said of Monk that he plays magnificent piano despite the fact that he's got no technique and Cecil Taylor says that is absurd. That is like saying Beethoven has got great technique, but he can't play Monk. You know, it doesn't make any sense to say things like that. Monk has the technique he needs to play Monk and you take it or leave it. That's it.

LANCASTER: Right. Like Beethoven had a technique but that's all he had.

SZWED: Right. One who played Monk with technique wouldn't be Monk. Monk takes long runs, he skips notes, and Monk is skipping notes because Monk skips notes.

LANCASTER: Well, I think that everybody can play. Just decide what kind of music you are going to play and what kind of instrument and when, and just use sincerity; but I think everybody has something to say. The same as talking. All you have to do is put the words into the musical instrument and the vocal thing or whatever is happening; but everybody has something to say.

SZWED: Did you ever try singing yourself?

LANCASTER: Yes. I sang a couple of times on a gig and I've been practicing every day. In fact, I have a tune right here that has words to it. I got the album last summer and it has the words to it and I've been singing that on a couple of gigs and I've been practicing everything.

SZWED: Do you remember when you first heard John Coltrane? That would have been with Monk or—

LANCASTER: '55?

SZWED: Yeah. It would have been with Miles afterwards. You heard him with Miles?

LANCASTER: Yes, of course, in person.

SZWED: And Cannonball Adderley. That would have been the first you heard him? That was when he was getting steam together.

LANCASTER: Yeah. He had it together then, you know. It was just something different that he was doing.

SZWED: What I'm talking about is the first time you heard him.

LANCASTER: Well, I always liked him; I always liked everything. Liked Ornette the first time I heard him and I liked Cecil the first time I heard him. I didn't really love it the way I do now. I listen to everybody. I still go back and listen to Brubeck and Desmond because I dig that. I listen to everything that is happening. Everybody who has something to say about jazz, which is one of the things that I am doing, I want to listen to. If they have something to say about money, I want to listen to them about that, too.

SZWED: What do you think turns off older jazzmen from Coleman or Coltrane? You know, they say, oh, man, just noise. What keeps them from getting into this stuff?

LANCASTER: Well, first of all, I don't think they should say anything, and most of the time they don't know what to say, because they're too busy playing their instruments and then they always change their minds most of the time after they check it out. After Coleman Hawkins heard Duke and Trane, like then he changed his mind. You know, a ballad and it was just what John Coltrane decided to play at that time, or with the help of Bob Thiele, maybe they have it. But I think most of the time when they say something, it's without knowing the guy. Because if they know the guy and he couldn't play at all, you know, they would say something nice about him if they liked him as a person. Most of the time we haven't known each other and we should spend more time knowing each other, before that, and when we know each other that may just get us together more and we can say what is and what isn't.

SZWED: Let's move on to the subject of the business, the music. One of the things that sets jazz apart from other kinds of music and people working together, is that jazzmen have been famous for the—you know—inside squabbles, the duels. I have heard rock musicians, soul musicians, say, look at those guys up there, every guy is struggling for his place and he's fighting, and his is the older stuff, you know, and here comes so-and-so up there and he's going to cut in and it's a fight every night. These guys are all personalities and they are ego-centered. But now, the new thing of rock and roll, here we are all together and so forth. Do you think there's anything to that kind of comment?

LANCASTER: One thing about the new music is that nobody can cut anybody, because you're all supposed to say what you have to say. And you should do it vibration-wise. In other words, you take a solo for the length of time that you would feel.

SZED: You think the idea of the older jazzmen was that there was a certain peak you could reach and there was a right way and a single way to go. Do you have a comment on that?

LANCASTER: Well, you know, there's a right way to stand in line. Everything influences everything and everything is everything, but now, we are trying to learn how to be men. I mean, everybody should be, but the new musicians are, because we have a lot to play and music has revealed a lot in seeking the Creator, which John Coltrane made very plain to everyone. So nobody cuts anybody and everybody's trying to help everybody which is—I hate to use the word Christian, but that type of idea, it's being Christian. Help somebody else, because when you help somebody else you help your self.

SZWED: I'll risk saying that I think this is what you are just saying. I think this is Afro-American style and we go back to churches in the South—the basic notion is that even though there is a preacher or somebody who is in charge, he's not that much in charge and he doesn't run things, you know, as in a white church. It's sort of a group thing. They have the self-help groups, not strictly in a church setting. The same thing happened in other ways. There were men's groups, like fraternities, burial associations, and so on. Cooperative is not quite the word that I want, but it's the thing that you find broadly across Afro-America and you don't find it in white America or even in a large part of Europe.

LANCASTER: Well, I discovered, which helped me a lot with the Steve Marcus Group and ourselves, everybody doing their share and turning on everybody else and different things. I find that quite a bit in the younger groups, because I think now is the time and now is the time for heaven on earth, which would be that way. If I give a student a lesson and he just has a dollar, then it's just as much as five dollars, if that's what he has, if he wants to give it to me. And if he doesn't want to give it to me, then he could bring me a bottle of wine and that would be cool, too.

SZWED: Well, do you think that in terms of getting together with the people in the music business, that you need some kind of new group, new association, or are you working OK as it is?

LANCASTER: Well, new group of what?

SZWED: Well, anything, whether it's a guild or whatever.

LANCASTER: I think we need a different kind of thing, with men becoming men, a thing that goes back hundreds of years and the people of the United States have been doing it and we don't know what was going on then, and if it was not going on then, then it's probably not going to go on until we do it ourselves. But also, I've put most of my value on myself and family this present time, in saying that I could perform by myself—a half hour, forty-five minutes, whatever it is playing quite a few instruments. Even if it was just on the saxophone, just like a violinist, classical violinist, or a cello player or anybody, a pianist like Van Cliburn or somebody. You know, I can do just as well or better and then you had to have the group—but you have to be able to take care of your home first, which I'm trying to be able to do.

SZWED: By the way, somebody said to me the other day, "But I'm talking about *serious* music," and I said, "Well, *I'm* talking about serious music." I am talking about cats who don't make a living at it and they keep playing, so you tell me anything more serious than that. Driving a cab in New York, while Archie Shepp is in the shipping department at a department store, and they're still playing. Roswell Rudd was driving a cab, and so you tell me anything more serious than a cat who is starving at music and I'll talk about it. He means, you know, serious people who are supported by universities.

LANCASTER: Yeah.

SZWED: But I see the time coming when the universities are going to support jazzmen. I feel that already at places like Yale, where they have had concerts and put out records and so on. The Lenox Music Barn. It really worked there and they even had a scholarship.

LANCASTER: You mean, in Massachusetts?

SZWED: Well, Herb Pomeroy was one of the teachers. He's already the best teacher. Like those things brought guys together and they brought Dizzy Gillespie up there to talk to these young cats who didn't understand. Let's talk about the finance field for a while. Jazz magazines, which have only been in this country for a short while—I mean, other than the collectors' magazines, which do not reach the masses—I never had much to do with them until the last few years. One thing I've learned, and it's a thing on which musicians are still not fully informed, it's a general feeling that the people who work with jazz magazines have made a living off of it and, as far as I can tell, only about five people in the history of the country have made a living writing about jazz.

LANCASTER: Leonard Feather.

SZWED: Leonard Feather has made three livings already talking about jazz.

LANCASTER: And there's George somebody.

SZWED: Simon. George Simon. But he wrote on big bands.

LANCASTER: Hoefer.

SZWED: No, George Hoefer didn't. He was an engineer and did it on the side. But there are a lot of names, like Don Heckman; he's a saxophone player.

LANCASTER: Yes. I met him. I went over to his house to talk about an article he wrote once. Talented.

SZWED: Well, these last few cats are not making a living. There are two points I am getting at by starting this way; not defensively, I don't want to sound defensive. But the point is, this is one point: should jazz magazines exist? And two, who should run them? Let's start it that way. Who should participate in them?

LANCASTER: Well, I think they should definitely exist, especially in the present-day system and eventually they wouldn't have to because there may be nothing to write about maybe fifty, sixty, seventy years from now. But like, right now, they have to exist because they already do. There are other magazines in other trades, just to help the trade. Let's think of it as a basic trade. And then, of course, you should have the critics and things like this, if they are really critics, so I would exclude most of them. They have to exist, because we wouldn't have time to do it for ourself. But occasionally—we want to get it out there that we're doing it. Different things could be put into the magazine to help the musicians more and most of them have hardly gotten along, or succeeded and most of them don't tell the truth. And the truth is the truth. And the other techniques are that the people have to spend more time in the field to find out what is really going on and they should have one or two writers who are really musically contributing, like Archie Shepp and somebody, you know, who can give an opinion. And plus, which is what happened to me with *Down Beat*, like print either what you're going to print or don't print it at all or ask the author's permission. They cut the last two paragraphs out of the article I sent in, and it was, like music, you know. The first paragraph was one theme and the last paragraph was the main theme and they cut the main theme out because it was sort of racial.

SZWED: Well, the situation that you're getting at is that the bulk of the people who have written about jazz have described what they heard. Not criticized, just described what they felt, which is all right, but if you do that well—the point is that they didn't do that well—and I think the best of this sort of person is Whitney Balliett of *The New Yorker,* who writes just as though this is his head. Now, when he says something, you know just how he responds to it and you can judge on that basis. For instance, he said of Coltrane when he first heard him, "He sounds like he's trying to eat too many peanut butter sandwiches at once." Now, on that basis, you can say, as I did, forget him, that's it, later for him. But other cats disguised themselves, so that what you get is that "Coltrane is not competent to play so-and-so." He made a mistake and has run up to a high E or something, which is disguised. You know, his basic idea is that Coltrane is not good and I'm going to tell you in another form. The guy had told you "I didn't like it" and that's straightforward.

LANCASTER: That's definitely wrong, because people should decide for themselves and all the critics should be able to say is the basic thing about the length of the tune, who is employed, and the basic technical facility that he might have had. We don't always use it. And the composition and variety and form and togetherness of the players playing it as a unit, instead of just five players playing it. That's all there really is to say, because when somebody does—especially somebody like John Coltrane doing something new and you have not even heard it—then there is no criteria to base it on. So all you can really say about the new records that John was doing is, this is definitely something new. There are a lot of screams that make no sense to me, but they say so, you know, and these screams are going on every day of our life. Car accidents, baby screamings, subways, things like that.

SZWED: Happy screams and unhappy screams. Sad laughter and happy laughter, the whole thing. You know, one of the great farces in jazz writing and in discussion has always been people describing the blues. They say, well, the blues are sad and when a cat is singing a happy blues they don't know what to make of it. Progressive jazz is a happy music. That's been the thing: blues, sad; jazz, happy. I don't know. What about the recording business?

LANCASTER: It's a racket. Seems like most of the cats have been cheated so long that we have to jump up to it and wake up to it in the best way we can, record it yourself or record with other musicians, and give everybody an equal share on it and if you have to use a producer, then use a producer and give him his share and the manager his. But the musicians should get more money than they have ever gotten, because even the guy in the record store gets more for my record than I do, and I go around from city to city pushing it and he doesn't.

SZWED: This is a problem with rhythm and blues, rock and roll, all young musicians have the same problem, because they're used. Even if you produce your own record, if you try to distribute it, you can be used badly.

LANCASTER: But you're definitely going to be used, unless you have the intelligence not to be used or just want to be used. You are going to be used from the kickoff, because basically it's a black music. After we get out of all these revolutions and things like that, then there is going to be a revolution in the music world, because if the black musicians got together now and we didn't get what we wanted to get and we were together enough to quit, then all these companies would fold overnight. But obviously, we are not together enough. But one day we will be and by that time, I hope that the companies give what is due, or to give us a better contract than they have been giving.

SZWED: Well, you know, I've always had the feeling that records carry jazz, because there are so many towns that cats come from that there was never a jazz band there. Little town in North Carolina.

LANCASTER: Well, I know, I lived in Raleigh for a year.

SZWED: Well, you know, I've always had the feeling that records years would go by without having a clue as to what is coming out in Chicago. I mean, how would Ornette Coleman ever come from Texas? You know, who's in Texas unless they had gotten some records. How did John Coltrane reach the West Coast when he did and all the rest of it? You know, it's the main tool that the jazzman has to talk through and to see what your friends are doing. The record is like a book, it's the stuff of this business. This is the way you write and this is your message. You mentioned something about bringing out your own records. Mingus did this and apparently didn't do badly as it's being carried by some of the big places, you know, that you wouldn't expect his records to be in. I'm a musician and I play—so that you mentioned before, the new awareness of everything, that you get with musicians today. Do you feel that they have a new kind of political knowledge?

LANCASTER: Oh, we definitely do. But getting back to the other thing, you know, the first shall be last and the last shall be first, and if they wanted to get together in a race and have the music, then the last ones to get in the line, we're the last to get in line starting with the music. So that we could have unemployment and could have places to go and rest, and could have that and this kind of insurance, and showers at a club and a big dressing room and these kind of hours and this kind of pay. You know, every other union has it but us. But I would just like to appeal to every musician who wants to get it together. We have to do it ourselves, and individually, as a family of musicians, or with your family, state, and country.

SZWED: Are you suggesting a new union?

LANCASTER: Well, I don't know about all of that because they need one, or they need to revive the old one, but it seems quicker to me to form a new one, and I was thinking about that because according to our statistics in the union paper, there are only about 10,000 or at the most, 20,000 musicians making their wages—you know, just playing music and most of those would be—if there is another 10,000 they would be classical, country and western, or rock and roll. They only come down to maybe a good 5,000 musicians playing jazz and getting most of the money because we all don't do that. So there's only about 5,000; if they unite, then it's a much smaller union and a much stronger union and it's much stronger music.

SZWED: One thing I mean to ask you before the tape runs out, the minority of jazz musicians have been white cats, although the majority of the moneymakers have been white cats, as you know, riding on the copies and so forth, but in the last so many years, of course, the situation has changed and I think that the black musicians are publicly now acknowledged. I may be wrong, with exceptions. But people like Miles are clearly big names, and I think it's clearly all black music and it's understood by the public as well as by the musicians themselves. Now I would like to ask you two things: One, how did the white cats who get into jazz—I'm not talking about those who are just slick and can copy some stuff, but those who really play well—how do they get into the black music field?

LANCASTER: Okay. Cut that off right there. Well, I think basically because they just dig the music and they see what the music can do for you. Not the real reason for playing it, but just because they want to, is the reason everybody does everything, because they want to and then they find out about it after they get into it. Like a marriage or a love affair or playing an instrument like I played the piano and lost interest for a minute. And then, if you are playing jazz, a white musician, well, the black man says, well, if you're dumb enough to want to try it and don't see that it's black music and we're holding the music behind because it is a black music, you know, I want to give you the best I can give you without giving you too much to give them. Because we see that you're sympathetic with the black musician. Then a lot of white musicians just love the cat that they dig; you know, a lot of players sound just like Roland Kirk or just like Elvin Jones, and they emulate them and luckily, they might find themselves by emulating somebody else, but a lot of times they don't. A good example is Bobby Katz, who sounded just like Elvin. He loved Elvin. I lived with Bobby Katz for a couple of years—a drummer—and now he is finding himself. Very few white players really come up with a rhythm sound, but when they do, you know, they really get it over. Like Paul Desmond. And Herbie Mann is the only white flute player that I heard with an entirely different thing happening and he's getting it over because what he says is himself and it appeals to the people who feel like that. When you say something, simebody is going to listen to you. The people who will listen to your thing will always come to hear you. If they do something in art or in writing or in pictures, then you will go and dig their thing. Because you dig them. Like, I was always for Peter Sellers. He would be out of sight. Then somebody else might not.

SZWED: Let me push this deeper. I read a thing by Norman Mailer and he said that he saw Sonny Rollins back in Chicago when nobody knew him. He said he (Mailer) had a bad sinus headache and that,

I swear on the Bible, Sonny Rollins cleared up his sinus headache within three minutes. He goes on with this, and he goes on to commit himself that he feels that no white man can understand the black man's problems in American and what he said made me smile because that is Mailer's particular way of seeing things. Then I thought of the implication; something that you said, that when the white man gets into the music, doesn't he also get into the life to some degree—of course we're talking of degrees now—doesn't he begin to share some of the basic spiritual values of the black man? In other words, can you ever copy just a music?

LANCASTER: Oh, you definitely can do that because I have seen it with Bobby Katz, but the biggest problem with white musicians trying to get into black music or white people trying to help black people in the civil rights, is that they will try to take the role of the black player or person and they forget that they have their own role.

But the few things you find in jazz that you dig, why you would find it in Japanese music or a Japanese woman or a Japanese cat, Chinese lady, so you have to grab that and go dig that because any family or any field, we are in the world family, and this is hanging a lot of these people up today. Especially, America is saying, well, we got the right answer, but everybody has a little bit of the right answer. Americans influence the Mexicans not to take a siesta, but how many people dig going to sleep in the afternoon? When you get up, it's five or six o'clock and you go swimming and do some other things; you know. Like you want a siesta around twelve, so why do we have to knock that out? Like, they didn't dig the Englishman for the tea, you know. Well, what is wrong with having it? Or the black musicians for playing all the time. You know, because it was so hot over there too, you know, in Africa. So these are all the parts and if we're going to get the world together, then it has to be the family first, you know, the basic family and we're saying that by the time you really develop as a person it's a world family and each person and each race has a job to do.

SZWED: Do you think then that jazz belongs—as LeRoi Jones suggested—in with other kinds of music—the whole thing at this point in time, or is it still separate?

LANCASTER: Afro-American music, which is jazz, is the strongest music in the world and it is accepted and the only reason why it isn't accepted here is because it is black and if we had the money that we are supposed to get—say, if Nat King Cole made the money that Frank Sinatra was supposed to make, then there would be too many rich black people, and then we would be more equal. Like, right after Reconstruction, something like that, you know, and jazz has only died—which I meant to mention before—since maybe the forties. It's not really dead, just on the way out, but we're coming back in now.

Chicago:
Winds of Change
by Will Smith

In the new jazz it has too often been a matter of where you play, not how you blow, that is the criterion—a politics of location, it seems.

It ought to be clear by now to devotees of the new music that some of the strongest, most inventive players are *not* products of the New York City milieu. Numerous original voices are being heard throughout the country, and world, for that matter.

Of particular interest in this regard is the Chicago scene and that city's cooperative Association for the Advancement of Creative Musicians (AACM). The Chicago climate has produced a body of talent largely uninfluenced by the supposedly innovative and often overrated New York players. The music created by Chicago musicians like Roscoe Mitchell, Lester Bowie, Joseph Jarman, Malachi Favors, Richard Abrams, Anthony Braxton, Maurice McIntyre, and others is at least as fertile and often superior to the N.Y.C. contemporaries.

But the New York cats continue to get the publicity and most of the available record and club dates (though that's not saying much since most of the New Yorkers also are starving or working day jobs). Still, it is the Chicago players who have suffered an almost criminal lack of recognition, especially when one considers the contributions they've been making in the development of meaningful musical expression. And now many of the best Chicago musicians, among them Mitchell, Jarman, Bowie, Favors, and Braxton, have gone to Europe because of the lack of work, money, and exposure—yes, that old story.

Chicago's new music, as an entity, is little short of amazing considering the city's rather mundane artistic situation. The Windy City's players have developed an approach to improvisation and composition which is more convincing, honest, clear, stimulating, and imaginative than most of the highly touted New York men. The Chicagoans have not lost sight of humor, silence, and dynamics, avoiding the seemingly endless and excessive outpourings of some of the "main men" from the Apple. In Chicago, it seems to be a music of deeper feelings, of textures, and of subtlety—an organic creation. And the rhythmic impetus which is so much a part of jazz has not been totally shucked as merely a "decadent Western interference."

Of course, one must remember that there's a basis for new music innovation in the city. Sun Ra's band spent much of its formative life in Chicago. Players of the caliber of John Gilmore,

Marshall Allan, Pat Patrick, Charles Davis, and James Spaulding came out of the area through Ra's band. Bassist Wilbur Ware, that unsung giant, and so many others have come from the city.

The ultimate expression of the Chicago music scene is the trio of Mitchell, Bowie, and Favors, a unit which has alternately functioned as the Mitchell Art Ensemble and the Bowie Art Ensemble (since the three moved to the Paris area in mid-1969 and have been joined by Jarman, the working group is known as the Art Ensemble of Chicago).

The Ensemble treats music as an open reference. Restrictions of style, schools of musical thought, and needless pleasantries are avoided and supplanted by directed energies, all-music interactions, and a reliance on improvisational insight. Total sound is taken as a point of emphasis, as is the joy of just making music.

Since the Ensemble often functions without a drummer, each member of the trio acts as a percussionist. That feature and the use of numerous "little instruments" (slide whistle, siren, harmonica, bells, kazoo, etc.) allow the group to project an immense coloristic range. The spiraling, shifting, sometimes wildly intense, sometimes silent musical melting pot defies category.

The Ensemble was the nucleus of Mitchell's first recording, *Sound* (Delmark DS-408), a strong and excellently varied sextet date from late 1966. With the trio were tenor saxophonist McIntyre, trombonist-cellist Lester Lashley, and drummer Alvin Fielder. Then came Bowie's *Numbers 1 & 2* (Nessa N-1), with Jarman joining the trio for the second side. This very highly rated album was released in early 1968. It was followed by the release in early 1969 of Mitchell's fantastic *Congliptious* (Nessa N-2). Mitchell, Bowie, and Favors each have an *a cappella* track on the album's first side and are joined by drummer Robert Crowder for the full-group work on the second.

The individual merits of the trio's members rapidly become evident. Multi-instrumentalist Mitchell is not just a vivid and original soloist, but a composer of considerable imagination and daring. Though Mitchell's main horn is the alto sax, he's equally proficient on soprano and bass saxes. Additionally, Roscoe can be found shifting to flute, clarinet, recorder, and numerous other instruments. He often seems most interested in delving into the potentials of sound colors, yet is able to convey lyricism, and has a firm grasp on jazz roots and conventional modes of playing. Enormous energy, a demonic, fun-house mind, and an emphasis on creating what is least expected are parts of a conception that places him among the top men on alto.

Bowie, a St. Louis product who is primarily a trumpeter but also most adept on Flügelhorn and harmonica, is of a somewhat different persuasion than Mitchell. Lester is equally involved in tonal color exploration, but in a more conventional sense. He's even more aware of the music's past, making use of stylistic devices seldom heard since the early stages of jazz—growls, half-valve work, blats, highly vocalized passages, and all manner of rich timbres. Bowie's humor can't be overemphasized and his overall solo capacity is undoubtedly one of the strongest in the music. By the way, he's married to singer Fontella Bass.

The Ensemble's bassist, Favors, is a perfect foil for the two hornmen. His rock-solid rhythmic strength and ability to provide the needed emphasis are paramount virtues. While he's generally not as involved in fun and games as Mitchell and Bowie, he is far from an unwilling participant. His hands are dynamite fast and his musical mind is on a level with the finest of players.

Of course, these men are not alone in the top ranks. Joseph Jarman is a major on several horns and a composer of distinction for both small and large groups. While his varying-sized units have not reached the consistent superiority of performance found in the Art Ensemble, Joseph's solo work is among the strongest on the scene.

Jarman's two albums, *Song For* (Delmark DS-410) and *As If It Were the Seasons* (Delmark DS-417), deal in a multitude of strengths. The former (from early 1967) features hard-blowing new music with Jarman on alto and soprano saxes, and recitation. With him in varying context are trumpeter William Brimfield, tenor saxist Fred Anderson, the late pianist-marimbist Christopher Gaddy, the late bassist Charles Clark, and drummers Thurman Barker and Steve McCall.

On the second record (from mid-1968), Joseph performs on alto, soprano, bassoon, fife, and recorder. He's again backed by bassist Clark (this time on cello and koto, too), drummer Barker, and singer Sherri Scott on the beautifully rich title track. For the second side, they are joined by Abrams on piano and oboe, flutist Joel Brandon, tenor saxophonists Anderson and John Stubblefield, trumpeter John Jackson, and trombonist Lashley for a striking, large-group interactive work which is far and away the most successful performance in that musical direction. *Seasons* and Mitchell's *Congliptious* are two of the superior recordings of 1969. Both are in the *must* category.

Another multihorn player on the Chicago scene is Anthony Braxton. While his album, *Three Compositions of New Jazz* (Delmark DS-415), is not entirely successful, Braxton will no doubt become a major player. Anthony, whose main horn is the alto, also plays soprano, clarinet, flute, musette, accordion, etc. With Braxton on the album (from early 1968) are LeRoy Jenkins, violin, viola, etc.; Leo Smith, trumpet, mellophone, xylophone, etc.; and, on the second side Abrams on piano, cello, and alto clarinet.

Braxton's most noticeable influence is Eric Dolphy, with slight touches of Coltrane. He reveals a far more personal style on a recent European record led by vibraphonist-pianist-bass clarinetist Gunter Hampel *(The 8th of July 1969,* Birth NJ 001), yet the strong Dolphy ties are still evident. Anthony plays alto, soprano, and contrabass clarinet on it, by the way.

The failure of Braxton's own album is that it lacks a rhythm section and thus has little impetus. The music is rather like the wanderings of contemporary "serious" composers—cold, detached, and somewhat static. Oddly, Braxton has said that his music is an avoidance of Western ideas, yet the result is quite clearly leaning in that direction. Part of the failing can be laid to the weak, European-oriented playing of Jenkins. Still, Anthony is quite good on the album.

By the way, Delmark is planning to release a second Braxton album in the fall of 1970 and it ought to be a considerable improvement over his first.

Abrams, one of the leading forces and founding fathers of the AACM, gave many of the organization's players their start in his ensemble, the Experimental Band, in the early sixties. Incidentally, Abrams (also known as Muhal) has worked with many of the major jazz players, was part of the original WJT Plus 3, and has been in tenor saxophonist Eddie Harris' group.

On Richard's first album as a leader, *Levels and Degrees of Light* (Delmark DS-418), he presents a rather dark, mysterious picture. The record (from late 1967 or early 1968) features mostly very strong music, but is afflicted with a terrible engineering job and an echo effect reportedly engineered into the recording.

The leader's piano and clarinet are abetted by alto saxophonist Braxton, violinist Jenkins, tenor saxophonist McIntyre, vibist Gordon Emmanuel, bassists Clark and Leonard Jones, drummer Barker, vocalist Penelope Taylor, and poet David Moore.

Some powerful solo and duet work by Braxton and McIntyre is made considerably less listenable by the poor recording quality. Abrams, always a dynamic piano voice, is tough throughout. His clarinet work on the title track falls into the category of sonic exploration.

A second Abrams album on Delmark also is due in the fall of 1970.

Tenor saxophonist McIntyre's debut as a leader, *Humility in the Light of the Creator* (Delmark DS-419), fulfills his dynamite promise. McIntyre, also on clarinet and into all kinds of hard voices, is joined by bassists Favors and Mchaka Uba, drummers Barker and Ajaramu (Gerald Donavon), and vocalist George Hines on the first side. Hines is not present for the second side and the ensemble grows by three—trumpeter-Flügelhornist Smith, pianist Claudine Myers, and John Stubblefield, this time on soprano sax. Maurice manifested a style on Mitchell's *Sound* a bit like Archie Shepp's. On the Abrams album, McIntyre showed signs of moving into wholly individual regions. These signs are realized in his own album. He also is heard in a far different context on an album by blues man J. B. Hutto.

A recent album with strong ties to the Chicago scene and the AACM is under the leadership of Melvin Jackson, bassist with Eddie Harris' quartet. *Funky Skull* (Limelight LS-86071) is soulful, generally exciting, and particularly strong during the tracks featuring AACM players. Roscoe Mitchell is heard creating fine bass sax backing, functioning in a flute duet, and playing a great, stormy alto solo. Trumpeter Bowie is fine and enormously humorous on several tracks. Other AACM players on the date are Harris' regular pianist, Jodie Christian, trumpeter Smith, trombonist Steve Galloway, and tenor saxophonist and flutist Byron Bowie (a brother of Lester).

Mitchell, Jarman, Bowie, and Favors left for Europe shortly after the sudden death of bassist Clark in the spring of 1969. Steve McCall, one of the finest contemporary drummers, has been in Europe for several years, working with numerous groups.

The Chicagoans moved into a house outside Paris soon after arriving and reportedly have been playing concerts (once sharing the stage with Ornette Coleman) and recording in several countries. The Art Ensemble of Chicago performed at the First Paris Music Festival, sponsored by Byg Records in late October of 1969. Braxton left for the continent a month or two after the others and was working with various groups. He also played in the Paris event as a leader. Anthony's associates, trumpeter Smith and violinist Jenkins, also were reported to have gone to Europe, but nothing about them has been reported at this writing.

Obviously the departure of many of the major players has hurt, but Chicago and the AACM continue to produce strong music. Abrams still leads his band and groups led by alto saxophonist Henry Threadgill, flutists Brandon and Wallace McMillan, and tenorist Stubblefield continue to function under the AACM banner. McIntyre is still in the city and so are tenorist Anderson and trombonist Lashley. And some new players from St. Louis, alto saxophonists Oliver Lake and Julius Hemphill and trumpeter Floyd LeFlore, have performed in concert in Chicago.

That the city will continue to produce musicians of great invention is, one supposes, open to question. It can only be hoped that the Chicagoans in Europe find success and maybe return home. One thing is sure. That hard wind remains in Chicago and it might just change your head someday.

Leon Thomas:
Spirits Known and Unknown
by Nat Hentoff

Writing of Leon Thomas' singing on Pharaoh Sanders' *Karma,* Will Smith in *Jazz & Pop* observed: "The voice projection of the lyrics is good and full, and leads to a wordless yodel sounding not unlike an American Indian call—the moaning of spirits known and unknown."

Smith had gotten to the essence of Leon Thomas' approach to expanding the capacities of the voice in the new music. Thomas is searching as far into himself as he can go for spirits known and unknown and is creating new dimensions of vocal expressiveness to bring these spirits—these feelings—into the experience of others.

Although Thomas has been a professional for a long time and has recorded with Count Basie and Mary Lou Williams—as well as with Pharaoh Sanders—his first album under his own name, with himself at its core, did not come into being until Bob Thiele recorded him for Flying Dutchman.

Before getting to Thomas' present vocal goals and imperatives, it's instructive to trace his jazz odyssey. Since he is surely at the edge of making his own substantial impact, it's useful to look into his own roots.

Leon Thomas was born in East St. Louis, Illinois, on October 4, 1937. Though his parents were not musicians, music was a vital part of the domestic ambience. Both sang in church choirs, and both liked to listen to recordings. "There were a lot of the old things around," Leon remembers. "Recordings going all the way back to Blind Lemon Jefferson."

As a boy, Leon's primary call, so he felt then, was to athletics. Proficient in baseball, basketball, and track, he saw himself in the future as a professional on the diamond or the courts. But he always liked to sing, too—with the school choir, with friends, by himself.

One Sunday afternoon, while he was in the tenth grade, Thomas went into a club for some Cokes and for the music. The fiery center of the proceedings was Armando Peraza, and eventually the youngster found himself on stand, joining in on conga drum and bongos. A local musician told Peraza, "You can beat this kid on bongos, but not on singing." Young Thomas was encouraged to return the next week to sing.

On stand then were Jimmy Forrest and Grant Green. Thomas sat in, this time as a vocalist, and among the intrigued listeners was disk jockey Spider Burke who had a weekly late-afternoon radio show on which he played and showcased "live" performances. Burke invited Thomas to the station, and the singer's unique, advanced method of scat singing—more fluid and faster than the traditional approach to jazz vocalese—quickly won him a substantial local following.

He was sixteen, and he was beginning to have different thoughts about his vocation. "I had to learn a new song a week," Leon says, "since I was on the air regularly and I'd also become a fixture at a local club. I worked with lots of different groups there, including Green and Forrest, and the Trio Tres Bien—before they became a quartet."

At the time, his influences included Billy Eckstine, Arthur Prysock, and B. B. King. ("My mother liked B. B., and we had his records around.") Then his younger brother brought home a record on which Joe Carroll, a skillful scat singer, performed with Dizzy Gillespie. "I found out," says Leon, "that I could do what Carroll was doing, but there was also that little extra thing that was my own. I wasn't sure what it was until later when I began hearing horn players like Coltrane."

Thomas enlarged his audience, winning contests, coming in third in a competition for the whole St. Louis metropolitan area. That same summer, a key event happened in terms of his development. Miles Davis was due at the Peacock Alley, and since Miles was a hometown boy, there was even more anticipation than would be expected in any case. The local connoisseurs were also looking forward to hearing Sonny Rollins with Miles, but Sonny had just gone on his first self-imposed sabbatical, and John Coltrane was sent for from New York.

"At first," Leon recalls, "nobody dug what Trane was doing. My brother did though. He said, "Hey, he's doing on the horn what you've been trying to do with your voice!" And he was right. Trane was running all those changes, as was I, and he was also into something else—new ways of using sound to get deeper expression. I heard him every night. I couldn't believe it, man, what he was doing. I was also inspired by the rhythm section Miles had then—Philly Joe Jones, Red Garland, and Paul Chambers. Especially Paul because he was so young. It was an inspiration to see him up there with Miles and he not being too much older than I was."

After being graduated from high school, Leon went to Tennessee State on a music and dramatic scholarship. "But I hadn't given up sports," he emphasizes. "I also went out for the track team." The pull of music at Tennessee State was strong, however. Les Spann was there doing graduate work. Also working around campus were Hank Crawford, Milton Turner (a Ray Charles veteran), and Lewis Smith (who had been with Horace Silver). "Those guys began to encourage me," Leon observes, "and my second year at Tennessee State was spent mostly on the road with a little group formed at the school. We worked Nashville, Kentucky, Alabama, and other places in that general area. When Hank left to join Ray Charles, the group broke up, and I went to work at the New Era Club in Nashville where I'd appeared from time to time before."

A number of musicians and singers passing through told Leon he ought to go to New York—*that* was the proving ground. "But Faye Adams," says Leon, "was the only one who really set some things up for me." On a lead from Faye, he came to New York in September 1958, to record for RCA Victor. The album was cut the next month, but was not released. "I was hanging around the Shaw booking agency," Leon adds, "and about ready to give up. But one day a slot was open at the Apollo when Austin Cromer was incapacitated. So there I was, with a chance to go on the same bill with Dakota Staton, an all-star big band led by Art Blakey, Ahmad Jamal, and Nipsey Russell. The agency wanted to know if I had arrangements. I told them I had, and thanks to Melba Liston working from Tuesday to Thursday, I did have some charts in time for rehearsal."

On opening day, Friday, Leon reached the demanding Apollo audiences so resoundingly that he kept being called back for encores. Blakey took a quintet from his big band on the road after that week at the Apollo, and Leon went along with them. "It was great experience," he points out, "and I kept meeting cats everywhere."

By 1960, when the black student movement for civil rights was emerging in the South, Leon decided to check things out back in Nashville at Tennessee State. His brother was a key force in the movement. "I stayed around a while," Leon says, "and got a gig in a local club. Count Basie came down for a spring dance, heard me, and told me to look him up if I ever came back to New York. Well, that next week, I was backstage at the Apollo. I ran into Joe Williams, who remembered me from that week I'd played at the theatre, and Joe told me he was getting ready to leave Basie." At Williams' suggestion, Leon called the Count, who gave him work at his Harlem club weekends until Williams did leave the band. Meanwhile he was also working at Café Wha in the Village with Booker Ervin, Richard Davis, and Jaki Byard.

Finally, in January, 1961, young Leon Thomas was in the big leagues —singing with Basie. It only lasted a month because he had to go into the army. "But I was in only six months, and then I worked around, getting myself together, until joining Basie again in 1963. I stayed with him for two years."

After that period, Leon broadened his experience through work with Randy Weston, Roland Kirk, Benny Powell, Joe Newman, and Tony Scott. The latter was at the Dom in the East Village for a considerable time, and it was here that Leon was first heard by Archie Shepp and Pharoah Sanders. "They used to come down on weekends," Leon notes, "and we got into some wild musical things."

There was also an important learning experience for Leon in Los Angeles for four months in 1967. "I worked with members of UGMAA—Underground Musicians and Artists Association. It was an extraordinary musical experience for me. They were really into the avant-garde, into freedom-type music. And I began to hear all kinds of possibilities as I got rid of a lot of prejudices I had had about the limitations of the voice. We were like a big Sun Ra family, and I learned a great deal from Horace Tapscott, who played piano, Black

Arthur, an alto player, Lester Robinson, who's on trombone with Gerald Wilson, and Leroy Brooks, a drummer. Leroy recently died; he was the Elvin Jones of *this* moment!"

Having learned to "stretch in all directions" while in Los Angeles, Leon came back to New York and in 1968 formed a natural alliance with Pharoah Sanders, with whom he has worked since, along with his own free-lance assignments.

Asked to describe the first album of his own after all these years of learning and exploring, Leon begins by pointing out that "some of it has to do with what you could call social commentary. It's a big task, but I'm going to try to help bring some order, some perspective into what's happening all around us now. And then part of it is basic jazz material. I like to write lyrics to originals like Horace Silver's "Song for My Father" and several of Trane's things.

"But through everything I do now," Thomas emphasizes, "there's my conviction that you have to be more than an entertainer. It just doesn't make any sense pretending nothing else is happening outside of wherever it is you're performing. But that doesn't mean a creative artist has to reflect chaos and disorder. It's the other way around. A lot of stuff is coming up in music that has nothing to do with art, but an artist can try to order what's going on while commenting on it."

The album also focuses on Thomas' further conviction that the time has come for the expansion of the voice in the new music. "In a way," he says, "things have come full circle. At the very beginning of all music, there was the voice. Now we're getting back to the importance of that primary human instrument. The voice can be the most evocative of all instruments; but as I hear things, for that to happen requires going into the most ancient forms of musical expression—what the pygmies and others sing in Africa. Indian ragas, music of the Himalayas. If you listen, although some people regard these people as 'primitives,' what they're doing is really very complex and subtle, but at the same time it's also a very free expression of the voice.

"They used to call me 'Mr. Modern,'" Leon smiles, "when I was doing that radio show at home. But I contend that to be really into what is modern, you have to simultaneously go as far back as you can. And in the process, as you liberate the voice, you find the voice can play a most important role in terms of talking about what's going on. People will listen to singing where they won't pay much attention to a speech. But to get them to listen, you really have to get at their *feelings,* and that means getting at your own.

"I call what I do 'egoless,'" Leon explains, "because it goes into the unconscious. It can be a moan or a cry or a tear. It can be a great big sigh—but under control. The thing is, however, not to be limited to what you consciously think or feel—you have to let it all well up. I have no label for what I'm doing; I guess there isn't any name yet for what it is."

So Leon Thomas, caring less about labels than about origins—of sound, of his own feelings—is building on all the years of listening and traveling and singing to create his own unmistakable sound and style. And he's also doing a lot of living. He's been married since 1962 to Lorraine, a girl he met at Tennessee State, and he hasn't lost his passion for sports. "I still play basketball all the time," he says, "with some of the baddest cats you can find."

But at the focus of the prodigious energy of Leon Thomas, 6′ 2″, with the stamina of an athlete and the drive of a creator, is his insistence that "we're into a new period. So far the horns have been in the forefront in terms of exploring the new dimensions of sound and expression. But no one has been nearly adventurous enough—for *this* time—with the possibilities of the voice. I feel I'm into that, and I feel it can be unusually therapeutic, for the listener as well as for the singer. All I need is a chance to get to the ears of the people."

That chance has finally come.

Archie Shepp: The Way Ahead by Nat Hentoff

I first saw and heard Archie Shepp in early 1959. Cecil Taylor brought him to a record date I was "supervising." Actually, with Cecil, the only "supervising" to be done was to tell him how long each take was. He knew exactly what he wanted in his music. As I remember, my initial impression of Archie's playing was that it was very powerful—the kind of intensity that wasn't manufactured, that came from far inside a man with strong feelings and an urgent need to get them out. I also thought at the time that his playing wasn't quite together, but then I wasn't entirely together in my own mind about what was happening in the "new jazz," or however you want to describe what has since become part of the basic jazz language of the 1960s.

In the years following, I watched Archie's development—both as a musician and as a trenchantly articulate critic of the contradictions and hypocrisies in American society. He wrote articles and plays; and when a critic would write something about his music that Archie thought obtuse, Archie would usually respond with a stinging rebuttal to the magazine in question. I dug that. For too long most musicians had not answered back, but now critics were being held directly accountable by the musicians themselves for the accuracy of what they said.

Of course, as a result of his determination to speak his thoughts and feelings candidly, Archie came to be considered "controversial" by some. I consider that term an honorable one, because without controversy, you may get order but you never get justice. Meanwhile he was also acquiring a larger and larger audience for his music. Not that work came easily or often in the States, but it did come from time to time, and his series of LPs for Impulse also added to his public.

In late 1967, Archie and his group toured Europe as part of a musical assembly organized by George Wein. He was heard in Denmark, Holland, Germany, France, Italy, Sweden, and England. There were some dissenters, but, in very large part, both audiences and critics were most impressed. Writing in the British *Jazz Journal,* Barry McRae described how Archie had brought a week in London of "assorted jazz attractions" to a "tremendous climax."

When he returned home, Archie was still buoyant about the reaction of European audiences. "I think," he said, "part of the reason for the success of the tour was the fact that it was imaginatively presented. There was a real diversity of groups. I'd been telling that to club owners in America for years. Diversify. Engage Cecil Taylor and Thelonious Monk together. Or Miles Davis and myself. Anyway, it certainly worked there. At Hammersmith on the British tour we sold out twice in one day."

The band came off that European tour really together, and although there was no immediate club work for it, Archie did make another album for Impulse, a label with which he had just signed a new extended contract. I asked him what directions he felt his music was going to take in the next year or so. "For one thing," Archie answered, "I'd like to work more and more with African rhythms. I'd like to take a trip to Africa soon, just look around, and absorb some of the contemporary folk material there as well as the older forms of music. It seems to me we have to keep developing a contemporary folk language. That's one of the reasons I listen very closely to rhythm and blues singers—the late Otis Redding, Wilson Pickett, James Brown. They exemplify what I mean by a contemporary folk language. We need more of that in jazz."

As he spoke, I remembered that a couple of years ago Archie had emphasized his conviction that jazz could reach a wide audience among the young as it got down to basic emotions in a folklike language. And he was especially interested in reaching the black young. He still is. "But," he adds, "we're kept out of communication with the black young. Look at those huge government expenditures for 'culture' in poverty areas. They give the money to teach the kids Shakespeare, but why not some of those funds for black music so that kids—and not only black kids—can see how deep and rich the heritage of that music is?"

Archie's own jazz reflects his concern for the full scope and history of the music. How, I asked, would you define the base of the jazz tradition? "Self-expression," he answered. "And a certain quality of human dignity despite all obstacles. despite the enslavement of the black man and then his oppression. And each of the great players has had so distinctive, so individual a voice. There is only one Bird, one Ben Webster, one Cootie Williams. That's jazz—the uniqueness of the individual. If he believes in himself, every person is not only different but valuably different.

"I think this uniqueness of the individual," Archie added, "is less operative in the so-called 'new jazz' because many of the younger players haven't had the chance to get enough experience relating to audiences. Nor has there been enough understanding by some of them of the whole jazz tradition. We all need deep relationships to the masters—Pres and Bird and the like—who led the way. That's one thing our group has, that sense of relationship. In Europe, we moved audiences even though we followed Miles Davis. And you know it's hard to follow Miles. But I'd spent a lot of time listening to Miles. I knew each of his periods, I know his tradition. So although we certainly played our own way, what we played showed our knowledge of what had preceded us—and an audience feels that."

I mentioned to Archie that a British journalist had written, "Shepp's playing has an immediacy that demands action," and that, accordingly, when he played at Ronnie Scott's club, there were people who couldn't keep themselves from dancing. "Yes," said Archie, "I'm always pleased when people dance. Jazz *ought* to be danced to. Don't forget music has always been a *performing* art—and that means in terms of the audience as well as the players. In the past, when people have felt jazz strongly, they've danced to it. There's no reason it shouldn't be that way now. And a player needs this added dimension of communication with an audience. It's a great feeling, a very graphic emotional sight, when an audience moves."

A while ago, Archie recalled, he and his band had played at the wedding of the daughter of film maker Shirley Clarke. "We'd been into a tune for forty-five minutes," Archie said, "when Jason, a man Shirley made a picture about, grabbed her and they started to dance. In a split second everyone was dancing. And you know, seeing and feeling them dance recharged us so that we played that tune for ninety minutes!

"That all makes sense to me," Archie went on. "It's part of the tradition I was talking about. I like it when people clap their hands and pat their feet to our music. And every once in a while we play in 4/4. Some of the so-called 'avant-garde' guys don't do that. They think it's passé. I don't. It's absurd to throw out everything from the past in order to be 'new.' If things from the past fit, you use them."

Thinking of the jazz past and of its future, I remembered what Archie had written about the present sounds of jazz in a New York *Times* article, "Black Power and Black Jazz": "This new statement has been accused of being 'angry' by some, and if so, there is certainly some justification for that emotion. On the other hand, it does not proscribe on the basis of color. Its only prerequisites are honesty and an open mind. The breadth of this statement is as vast as America, its theme the din of the streets, its motive freedom."

In our conversation, I asked him to elaborate. "The underlying symbolism of jazz," Archie said, "has always been black, and so have been the great innovators. But jazz is accessible to all people, if they're honest enough to receive it. Roswell Rudd in our band is an example of that. It's an honesty that's necessary not only in jazz, but with regard to the most crucial problem in America—the racial problem. Most whites have allowed the relationship between the races to deteriorate, but there are some who are honest about what has to be done and who do see the need for profound and meaningful change in this country to end racism. But there's so much distance now between the white and black worlds, so much noncommunication. And yet if that problem isn't solved, the future is, to say the least, very bleak."

And what of Archie's own future? "As rough as it may be economically, I'm going to keep the band together as best I can. And we'll keep recording for Impulse." Archie also remains active as a playwright, having recently completed two one-act works, *Skulls* and *69*. He had taught in the schools for a while. Would he ever do it again?

"Not in the schools as they are now," Archie answered. "The only kind of teaching I'd like to do is in a school I'd build myself with the kind of curriculum which allows for creative teaching and for learning in a natural environment."

What of the future of jazz? "It must return to the ghetto where it began," Archie emphasized. "We have to reach the kids and become part of the whole cultural experience, the whole history out of which jazz came. But again I wouldn't limit the experience of the music to ghetto children. White kids also need to know what jazz has to say if they're going to live in a real world."

It is this sense of reality that particularly characterizes Archie's music. As in all the best jazz, the music is an extension of the man. And as a man, Archie addresses himself to the totality of experience in his life. He is an intellectual who does not shut off emotion. Quite the contrary. He is black, and proud of being black, and he is an increasingly important communicator—in his music, in his articles, in his plays—of black consciousness.

In writing about the change in the music of the American black man as he became more and more urbanized, Archie also writes about himself: "As the tempo of life increased, all art reflected the change. People walked faster. Notes were played faster. New hopes were born and, like the tall buildings of cities, they seemed to reach to the sky. The children of the previous generation were now grown up and were challenging the democratic process to provide solutions instead of academic inquiries. They were not going to be put off with the same old lies, not about to be hacked to death on their knees."

I don't know what's going to happen with regard to the black-white division in America. I do know that Archie Shepp is one man who is going to keep telling us what he feels—without dilution—in his music and in everything else he does. And you'll never see him on his knees. I also know that the music, like the man, will continue to grow and surprise and provoke listeners into further explorations of their own emotions, their own definitions of what life is about. Like all durable jazzmen in the tradition, Archie is unmistakably unique. But also like them, his basic concerns are universal and elemental—freedom, dignity, honesty. And that's why his music has such seizing force. It gives you no place to hide.

Alice Coltrane
Interview by Pauline Rivelli

(Alice McLeod Coltrane was born in Detroit, Michigan, August 27, 1937. Coming from a musical family, she studied with private teachers and worked locally with a trio. She spent a year on the road with Terry Gibbs (1962–63). Mrs. Coltrane replaced McCoy Tyner in the John Coltrane quartet in 1966. Alice and John Coltrane met on July 18, 1963, were later married, and had three sons.

The following interview took place on Saturday, July 13, 1968—almost a year after John Coltrane's death, July 17, 1967.

Sitting with Alice Coltrane in her home, one could actually feel the presence of John Coltrane. Surrounded by his children, John, Jr. (who looks exactly like his father), Ravi, and baby Oranyan, a feeling of great love permeated the air. Spiritually, John Coltrane was there, too. A huge, golden harp sat next to a concert grand piano; drums and cymbals, bells, and gongs were about the room, reminding us of John Coltrane's explorations in sound.

The quiet dignity of Alice Coltrane, the tranquility and graciousness of her home, confirmed the belief that John Coltrane truly left a great legacy to those dear to him—peace and love.)

PAULINE: Who in your family back home in Detroit was musically inclined?
ALICE: My mother played piano and sang in the church choir. My brother is a musician, Ernie Farrow, bassist.
PAULINE: Do you consider yourself a jazz pianist—would you classify your music as jazz?
ALICE: No. The use of the term, I feel, is inadequate in its description of the music created through John. A higher principle is involved here. Some of his latest works aren't musical compositions. I mean they aren't based entirely on music. A lot of it has to do with mathematics, some on rhythmic structure and the power of repetition, some on elementals. He always felt that sound was the first manifestation in creation before music. I would like to play music according to the ideals set forth by John and continue to let a cosmic principle, or the aspect of spirituality, be the underlying reality behind the music as he had.
PAULINE: Did John Coltrane rather not use the term jazz? How did he classify his music?
ALICE: He didn't classify it as anything. He seemed uncomfortable when using the term. A few years ago—about three years—I asked him, and only for my own interest before I started

playing—in fact, I wasn't playing at all. I asked him what it was that he was doing in music. These are his exact words: he said, "I am looking for a universal sound." At the time I didn't quite understand him fully, but I think what he was trying to do in music was the same thing he was trying to do in his life. That was to universalize his music, his life, even his religion. It was all based on a universal concept, all-sectarian or nonsectarian. In other words, he respected all faiths, all religious beliefs. In music it was the same way too, because he had such a combination of concepts and ideas, some interwoven with each other. He was doing something with numbers once; he was doing something from a map he drew—sort of like a globe—taking scales from it, taking modal things from it. And he was continually changing and continually doing things like that, and another day it would be something else. Working with harmonics, working with chromatics, microtones, working with overtones, adding octaves to his instrument. I think this is what helped me in my music. John showed me how to play fully. In other words, he'd teach me not to stay in one spot and play in one chord pattern. "Branch out, open up, play your instrument. You have a whole left register—use it. You have an upper register—use it. Play your instrument entirely." These are the things he taught. I really think that helped me to understand myself. It was perfect.

John not only taught me to explore, but to play thoroughly and completely. Not as musicians played years ago. They played on chord changes when they played thirty-two-bar music or twelve-bar music; everything was kind of on a limited basis. They couldn't go outside the chord changes and they had to fall in right on the beat, you know. You have got to stress the freedom of music to really branch out and be universal. It was a higher concept John had. It was higher than this world's.

PAULINE: Up until the time of his death, was John still searching or exploring new sounds? Or was he satisfied with the sounds he had mastered through his years of experience?

ALICE: I don't think John was ever satisfied with his music, to tell you the truth. He was never satisfied completely. He did have moments of happiness and satisfaction—but only momentarily. Then he'd be on to something else again.

PAULINE: Do you find that in your music, you're doing the same thing? Are you exploring and broadening and searching?

ALICE: I don't think that I have the talent of my husband. I don't have the genius of John, but I will try to elevate the music as much as I possibly can.

PAULINE: John Coltrane seemed to have had a secret of some kind. We'd all love to know his "secret"—or message. No one seems to know.

ALICE: Right, right. Because no one, as yet, has been able to reach up to the things he tried to do. The man gave so much. This is a clue. He did work on his music day and night. This is the truth. Day and night. Even when he wasn't practicing or actually working at his music, he'd be thinking about it.

PAULINE: He was happy doing it. It wasn't a chore—this is what he wanted to do.

ALICE: Yes, this is what he wanted to do. But how many people can devote that kind of time? Even if you like it. I like it but I still have responsibilities to my children and household, but John gave it his full undivided attention.

PAULINE: How long do you practice at the piano each day?

ALICE: I usually practice at night because during the day I'm busy with the children and can't really concentrate. But at night, at eleven or twelve o'clock, I practice the piano, listen to tapes, practice the harp.

PAULINE: How many hours do you devote to the harp?

ALICE: Well, I practice a good hour.

PAULINE: Is the harp self-taught?

ALICE: Yes. John wanted a harp in the family about two or three years ago.

PAULINE: Did John practice the harp? Did he intend to use it?

ALICE: Well, here's how it came about. He was using the harp for some of his studies and that's how the harp got into the family in the first place. He used it for his own music. You know, just like he did with other instruments—the bass clarinet, drums, things like that.

PAULINE: He just decided to get a harp and explore with that instrument too. Did he take lessons or have a "how to" book to guide him?

ALICE: He had a book he referred to in regards to tuning and things. He used to tune it his own way, though. Sometimes he'd just leave it because he said he liked to hear the air, if it was blowing through the house, just passing over the strings. The harp then gave out its own sounds. John liked that. He'd say that's a beautiful thing.

PAULINE: One of John's favorite projects was the furtherance of music through the discovery of new, young musicians. I understand this ambition will be furthered primarily under your guidance. Your own recordings have featured Jimmy Garrison, Rashied Ali, and Pharoah Sanders—all part of John's last recording group. Do you intend to record with anyone else—some new names?

ALICE: I would like to. I would like to do things with different musicians.

PAULINE: Do you have anyone in mind at the moment?

ALICE: No I don't, other than Joe Henderson. He's a good musician, and excellent in the field of orchestration. I want to do some things with him involving other instruments, strings and things like that. That's what I'd really like to do next.

PAULINE: With out-of-town concerts and tours, tours sometimes taking you out of the country, isn't this going to be difficult for you what with the children and running the household? How will you handle it?

ALICE: Well, I'll have to meet that when it comes. I'm not planning on that right now. I would like to concertize occasionally. But to really work like John did—that's something to which I'll have to give a lot of consideration.

PAULINE: Regarding concerts. You're referring to the type concert you gave this year on Easter Sunday at Carnegie Hall?

ALICE: Yes. And I'd very much like to play for students at college concerts, and churches, if they'll have me.

PAULINE: Speaking of students, do you have any advice to students regarding furtherance of their music? Is there any advice you can give to student musicians who really want to make it as professional musicians?

ALICE: Well, there are two approaches I think. First of all he can go ahead and get the background through study. Study classical music and contemporary music; blues and spirituals; find a good teacher; and get a good knowledge of his instrument, so that the student can control it. If he wants to go back in time and study other masters' works that's fine, in order to bring himself up to the music of today— like the music of my husband's—that's okay. I'm not against it. I think that's a good idea. But, with a good knowledge of his instrument, control, feeling for the instrument, and absolute mastery over it, he can start right now—as music is today, with the concept of John, the concept of Ornette Coleman and Cecil Taylor. The student can start right here, at this point, with his music.

PAULINE: Many young pop musicians today admire, respect, and are influenced by John Coltrane. Do you dig pop music at all?

ALICE: Well, I'll tell you. I like music—all kinds of music. I like some folk music. It is expressive, I like *all* religious music; I like Igor Stravinsky; I like Indian music; I like what the the African people play—rhythmically, I like what they're doing.

The thing I like about music is if the person likes what he or she is doing, if they have a strong conviction behind it, I don't care what they're doing—if they have a conviction behind it, then I appreciate and respect it. Because it's something that's flowing from their hearts. You know how you feel when you know someone is playing something that they really don't feel and really don't have their hearts into. You get the message—you like it but you don't really enjoy it. You really know the person wasn't truly giving his all.

PAULINE: People loved John Coltrane for the reason that they know he was giving his all. It wasn't just playing without feeling. The young pop musicians and young listeners knew this. Many pop musicians are Coltrane-influenced. They really dug Coltrane.

ALICE: Well, I like them when they put their whole hearts into the music, that's all that matters to me. I like all kinds of music on that basis, including hymns and anthems, gospel music, and music from the sanctified church. I do wish for the day, though, when all music, all phases of music under their various names and forms are transmuted and sublimed. This is the ultimate aim too, I believe, not only in music, but for all arts and sciences as well.

PAULINE: In closing, Alice, is there anything else you'd like to say to our readers?

ALICE: Well, the only thing I can say is that I know—I *know*— how badly John wanted to do this work.

PAULINE: Will you continue this work?

ALICE: I'm going to try. To do my best to do the things John wanted done—to reach the people.

PAULINE: In reaching the people what type message do you want to communicate through your music?

ALICE: Well, I don't know exactly how to put it. But everything I do is an offering to God—that's the truth.

PAULINE: That was John's commitment too. We know this especially through *A Love Supreme*. You realize, of course, that people may look to you as an extension of John Coltrane. At this point we both agree that no one can take the place of John Coltrane. However, what is your ultimate goal in carrying on John's work?

ALICE: The work I am trying to do is a sort of sharing with my sisters and brothers of the world, my all; the results I leave to God. I am really not concerned with results, my only concern is the work, the effort put forth.

PAULINE: How about the skeptics who refuse to recognize the truth? What if the truth does not set them free?

ALICE: Well, it will set *me* free because this is the work *I'm* committed to do myself, you know. In other words, if I give you a leaf or a pearl that you trample in the dust, then I am sorry. I give them to you because I want to. It is my gift—my offering—to you; you do with it as you wish.

Afterword

Now, of course, it is regarded as an authentic jazz style. Though it claims, in its pristine incarnations, an audience roughly equal in size to that of the Seattle Mariners, it is acknowledged as a legitimate music. Musicians working in other forms (in modern "concert" music and rock as well as jazz) express respect for its techniques and reveal its influence. The entertainment listings of the weekend newspapers actually propose it as an agreeable option for a Saturday night—should a "challenge to hard and serious listening" be your mood. One may even hear, occasionally, interpolations of certain of its characteristics and mannerisms in popular musics intended to function as an anodyne or soporific; in a saxophone passage or ensemble movement on an airplane cassette or on the Tonight Show. And, indeed, Cecil Taylor was recently invited to play for a President.

Certainly no one who "lived tight" with the "New Black Music" in its early days, and who defended it against what must have been the most vehement critical reaction to be evoked by any music since the premiere performance of "The Rite of Spring," could fail to take a large measure of satisfaction from the vindication of its radical departures. But, just as certainly, for those of us who remember what this music wanted to be about, and who were fervently caught up with its ambition, any satisfaction derived from its passage into the mainstream of jazz and American culture has to be edged with melancholy.

As a self-described projection of the philosophies of Black Cultural Nationalism, it was not, after all, the original desire of "free jazz" to gain entrance into the Western musical establishment; or, indeed, to infuse prevailing Western popular or even "art" musics with new blood and new choices. In its rejection of Western musical procedures—avowedly a rejection of the technocratic sensibility which had conceived them—and with its assertion of what Cecil Taylor called "ancient Black Methodologies" (notably collective improvisations), the "New Black Music" was aspiring to be nothing less than an embodiment of a new culture, a culture that would grant trust and primacy to the life-ordering and life-enhancing resources of spirituality.

But despite the irony of its current status and my own nostalgia for the high fevers and visionary passions of the sixties, the music has survived and we can take no small consolation from this fact. Even divested of its revolutionary mystique and ebullience it remains one of the most stunningly beautiful musical expressions to be heard anywhere. Taylor and Ornette Coleman go on and continue to "discover the marvelous," and Archie Shepp, last time I caught him, was playing like he was in love. Sunny Murray and Sun Ra and Andrew Cyrille are still around and they are developing and refining their esthetics. Meanwhile, new musicians are coming up who want to keep the line alive.

If we couldn't rush the millennium, we shall at least have something worth listening to while we wait for it.

ROBERT LEVIN
New York City
December, 1979